Gifts
From a Feral Cat

A Story of Love, Loss, and Miracles

Tian Wilson

good guest
publishing

Published 2022 by Good Guest Publishing

IBSN (Paperback): 979-8-9872385-0-9
IBSN (eBook): 979-8-9872385-1-6

Copyediting by Dustin Bilyk @ www.authorshand.com
Cover design by Craig Gundry

Inquiries should be addressed to: tian@tianwilson.com
www.tianwilson.com

Creative Non-fiction: This is a work of creative non-fiction. The story is portrayed to the best of the author's memory. Names, events, and details have been fictionalized in varying degrees for various purposes, including dialogue and characters. Location, timeline, and the cats involved are true. Some identifying characteristics have been changed to protect the anonymity of those involved.

The author in no way represents any company, corporation, or brand mentioned herein. The views expressed in this book are solely those of the author.

For The

Wordsmith, writer, and voracious reader
who cautioned me
to not dangle my participles...
Thanks, Mom

Contents

Gifts
From a Feral Cat

A Story of Love, Loss, and Miracles

1

Enchanted

"There are only two ways to live your life. One is as though nothing is a miracle. The other is as though everything is a miracle."
– Albert Einstein

In a world where proof is required to believe, I experienced the unbelievable.

My life had been built on logic—simple cause and effect. It was explainable. It made sense. And what didn't make sense was given a cursory nod and set to the side.

But as time moved along its silken stream, I discovered that some experiences have no explanation. They simply occur, without research to back up the observation, a published paper to validate the event, or authorities to give it their blessing.

That leaves me, if I can relinquish the need to prove everything, with a deep sense of wonder and mystery. And looking at the world as a mystery is both humbling and disconcerting.

This is such a story—magical and incomprehensible. It is a true story, even though names were changed, as were characters, conversations, and timelines. But the essential story and location are accurate.

Most importantly, the cats were real. They lived. And *their* story is true.

This is a "Teaching Story." I was the student, and the cats in their ancient, feline wisdom were the teachers. Their lives stimulated conversations with others who then added their own wisdom to this living classroom: my elderly neighbors, Gus and Emma; my tall, soft-spoken Navajo friend, Jake; and the spry Doc Parsons, the most perceptive person I've ever known.

At the heart of what I am about to tell you are unexplainable events that challenged my understanding of life. Inadvertently, they also deepened my connection to something infinite. There are many words that describe what I experienced—magical, inconceivable, mystical. But the best word I have found is "miraculous."

A miracle is defined as "a surprising and welcome event that is not explicable by natural or scientific laws." My experiences fit the definition. They could not be explained. By anyone.

This is the story of a series of extraordinary events from 1986 through 1990 that reawakened a long-dormant sense of precious amazement I had lost many years before.

When I was a child, I was open to Life, connected to the living things and a Creator that spread its banquet before me, beautifully laid out in sights, sounds, tastes, sensations, and feelings. I was comfortable not knowing and not understanding because my silent partner was ever-present to guide me in the exploration of the world. Without question, I knew I was loved by more than people.

My mother said I lived in a state of perpetual wonder, wide-eyed and open-mouthed in an expression of endless surprise. The world took my breath away, whether a jeweled butterfly emerged from its dry husk, a cut finger healed without a trace, or trees mysteriously changed their color overnight. Everything was magical. Everything was wonderment.

As I grew older, a kind of amnesia began to set in. I forgot that my mother's cool hand healed a fever, or that lightning bugs awoke at twilight to dance to a drumbeat only they could hear. I forgot how extraordinary life was. Little bit by little bit, I simply forgot my connection to the world around me.

At home and school, Growing Up meant to be responsible. Growing Up's job was to collect information, remember it, be smart, adept, and capable. These traits had far greater value than admitting, "I don't know... I'm amazed... I don't understand..."

There was no reward for *not* knowing. Answers were important, not questions. So, I crammed myself full of information to avoid the embarrassment of poor grades, or not being able to answer, not being able to explain, and not looking competent. My continuous childhood prayer of gratitude devolved into, "Whatever the cost, dear God, don't let me look ignorant."

As I struggled to fit into new groups, new responsibilities, new attitudes, the world lost its sheen and the amnesia deepened. I entered the world of adulthood, following the siren song that beckoned me to grow up, fit in, and don't stand out unless you know more, not less.

I was lost. Amnesia complete.

It was in this state of amnesia that I got married in the early 80's. By 1985, my husband and the knowledgeable adult I had become moved from the Midwest to Texas for a fresh start. Like many before us, we thought a change of scenery, a new job, new home, and new people would help us get back to "normal" and fix our differences. And like all who came before us with the same illusion, it worked for a while.

Until it didn't. What I *did* learn along the way was that when life wasn't working, it let me know in its loudest outdoor voice. In one painful year, I lost my husband, my job, my home, and my adult understanding of how life worked. He wanted to stay. I wanted to run away. So, I packed everything in a U-Haul and moved less than a year after I arrived. I was lucky. When our assets were split, I had enough to allow me the time I needed to figure out the next chapter in my life. To remember how to take deep breaths.

Though I'd lived in many areas of the country, I had never felt fully at home anyplace. Possibly because I had never felt fully at home inside myself. But when I arrived in New Mexico, aptly called The Land of Enchantment, it was like a dose of smelling salts for an unconscious life. I began to wake up and remember a time when I was connected to the mystery and beauty around me.

I fell in love like a child, accepting everything and finding fault with nothing.

I was drawn in not just by the people, but the explosion of new colors, sights, sounds, smells, and tastes. The vast open spaces soothed my soul. The mountains felt like gentle arms encircling me. I was thoroughly and completely charmed. And the amnesia began to lift.

Immersed in an unfolding history, I met those who were part of this melting pot: the Pueblo Indians; The Navajo or "Diné," which means "The People"; the Apache Tribes; the Mexican and Spanish people. I felt a surprising connection to *la gente de la tierra* (the people of the land). Alongside their ancient cultures, almost every ethnic background was represented, including we *bilagáana*, the Navajo word for Caucasians.

I was delighted by the sheer variety of color that permeated the landscape. During Balloon Fiesta, hundreds of vibrant hot air balloons floated in the pre-dawn skies like fat, blinking Christmas lights. Women's wildly colorful, spinning fiesta skirts flounced with the texture of multi-layered cotton candy during celebrations. Pottery, sand paintings, blankets, and jewelry seemed to glow, rich in colors of the land. Sunsets gleamed in layers of burnished copper, cottony pink, and deep grey as the Sandia Mountains were lit by a surreal watermelon color. Not since childhood had my mouth hung open and my eyes become huge in that long-forgotten expression of endless surprise.

I drank it in—soft rose, bruised purple, and every shade of umber, gold, ochre, and silver. These colors intertwined with the startling green of firs, sage, and bunch grass against the lofty, gentle mountains. It didn't just feed my eyes; it fed my spirit.

The weather was perfect—low humidity with cool nights and warm days. I lived in the high desert area of Albuquerque, miles from the lower Rio Grande Valley. Doors and windows were flung open in the evenings as we thumbed our noses at mosquitoes that avoided the dry air. Winters were gentle, an inch of snow causing the city to pause until the sun forced the powdery white fluff into happy puddles.

New fragrances surrounded me from season to season. During late summer and early fall, the smoky-sweet perfume of roasting chilies comingled with the musty fragrance of cottonwood leaves as I walked by the river. In winter, night winds brought the pungent, piney scents of mesquite wood and piñon smoke. Spring and summer offered the indescribable smell of creosote that permeated the air after a heavy rain. Year-round, the yeasty aroma of dense round loaves of bread from outdoor *horno* ovens made my mouth water. The perfume of food, flowers, trees, and land filled me.

The earth was generous, giving freely of sand, silt, and clay to form adobe, the backbone of southwest buildings. Structures felt organic, as if they grew from the earth to blend with the landscape. Rough-textured interior and exterior walls were peppered with beautiful flaws, slight bulges, and faint dips.

I walked through countless neighborhoods, marveling at the architecture. Some homes were surrounded by *latilla* fences made of unstripped saplings placed vertically like uneven soldiers frozen at attention. Other homes had adobe garden walls that formed an irregular barrier, delighting the eye in its fluid solidity. In the emergence of my fourth decade, I learned imperfection was beautiful.

When invited into my friends' homes, I was surprised by Talavera sinks and tiles in dazzling ochre, cobalt, yellow, and green.

These decorated tiles became counters, shelves, and stairs that integrated into every room of a home. Above me, ceilings had great *vigas*, beams made of tree trunks scraped bare of bark and used as visible support or decoration. Sometimes, hand-scraped *latillas* were laid between vigas to form intricate chevron patterns on ceilings. I was lifted by the natural beauty.

Some interiors also had indoor fireplaces, called kivas, that pushed out into rooms like a pregnant woman's belly. Everything felt soft, round, and feminine. Doorways were arched like beautiful eyebrows. Even floors of Saltillo tiles were made of good red clay that began its life soft and malleable inside Mother Earth. I thought of it then, as I do now, as a gentle architecture.

For the first three years, my two cats, Deidre and Cochon (sometimes called "Cush"), and I lived in a cramped and noisy one-bedroom apartment near a street that never slept. In 1989, after three years of apartment living, I began to feel overwhelmed by the transience of people, the thin walls, and the constant street noise. I found myself driving to Cibola National Forest, or Bandelier, or any area away from people. Driving back to Albuquerque, I would already be missing the open spaces and hushed solitude. So, I decided to look for something a little bigger and a lot quieter.

My girlfriend, Maureen, invited me to her home located south of the city. Any invitation to get out of the cramped apartment was met with open arms. Veering off I-25 S onto 47, I followed the two-lane road past the Isleta Reservation into the sleepy village of Bosque Farms. The "downtown" was two miles of feed store, bank, laundromat, small restaurants, a gas station, and other necessities of rural life. She had a lovely little home, a young son, and one sheep named Scrappy, what she called her $90 lawn mower investment for the weeds in the sprawling yard.

After hours of talking and coffee, we took a walk through her neighborhood. Our tennis shoes crunched on the gravel. I heard a few birds, some children laughing, and a car starting in the distance. The lack of noise was jarring. I turned to her, almost whispering, "It's so quiet."

"Why do you think I moved here?" She grinned. "We have everything we want and nothing we don't. It's a great place to raise my boy. We can take peaceful, year-round walks along the ditch banks, and even in town there's no heavy traffic." She waved her hand toward the surrounding homes. "My neighbors are salt of the earth. This is a community of sheer goodness. And we have Benny's."

"What's Benny's?" I asked.

"Some of the most delicious Mexican food in the southwest, smothered in the best green chili sauce I've ever had. I could bathe in it." We both laughed and decided we'd eat there before I headed back.

Benny's Mexican Kitchen, established in 1972, was everything she said and more. The people were welcoming, the service fast, helpings were generous, and the prices were fair. We both savored enchiladas smothered in homemade green chili sauce. My tastebuds stood at attention in celebration status.

As we talked, I told her I'd decided to move to someplace quieter. Dabbing her mouth with a paper napkin, she asked, "If you want some peace and quiet, have you thought about moving here? You're twenty minutes from Albuquerque if you want to go to the symphony or visit friends. You know my sister and her husband live down here, right?" I nodded. "They've outgrown their house and just bought a bigger one. They're renovating their small one for a rental."

The seed was planted.

That October, the cats and I moved to the farming community of Bosque Farms. My dream of living in a true adobe home was fulfilled when I rented her sister's beautifully restored, two-bedroom house in the heart of the Rio Grande Basin. It had a double lot with a big yard and was set off by itself at the end of a short dead-end street. It had farmland on all sides except one where my new neighbors, Gus and Emma, lived. It was an old, settled neighborhood, occupied by the same ten families that had lived there for over twenty years.

I was surrounded by hushed beauty—mountains, open fields, and irrigation canals called *acequias*. I was serenaded by the whisper of wind in cottonwood trees, distant coyote calls, and morning birdsong. It was heaven, especially after living in a noisy apartment complex.

Though less than twenty minutes from Albuquerque, it felt like I'd moved a hundred miles away. Instead of gazing out at the Sandia Mountains, I gazed at the Manzano Mountains to the east. I moved from Bernalillo County to Valencia County and the change was profound. This small, rural village of about 3500 people sat in the flatlands between the meandering Rio Grande on the west and the upward sloping plain toward the Manzanos in the east. The river made large swaths of the land nutrient-rich and verdant.

It was a riparian habitat in this arid state, a welcome wetland that provided a perfect environment for water-seeking plants and wildlife. Near the river and *acequias*, the soil was a natural home for alfalfa, beans, corn, chiles, and a multitude of grasses. Instead of kids on skateboards, I watched horses, sheep, and fat cows grazing in fields. It was a place that reminded you to slow down.

It was a good place for miracles.

So, how *does* one share something that makes no sense in our world? As I recall the events during that time of my life, they feel almost impossible to describe. But please join me and read the story of one strange and magical cat that changed my life forever.

2

Liberated

*"Do not neglect to show hospitality to strangers, for thereby
some have entertained angels unawares."*
– Hebrews 13:2

We met in the early morning on Thanksgiving Day, 1989. The dawn
was crisp with the chilly night air clinging to the warmer, small
breezes coming off the Bosque. The 22-pound turkey was stuffed
and cooking in the old Nesco roaster. The sweet, heady aroma of
pumpkin and apple pies filled the house with tantalizing promise.
Ten pounds of potatoes were peeled, covered with water, and
standing by in a big stockpot. It was only 7am.

Still in a robe, I stepped barefoot onto the cold, wooden deck,
softly closing the heavy door behind me. As I warmed my hands on
the steaming coffee cup, my chest filled with a deep breath of the
rich smells of New Mexico at dawn... lingering smoke from piñon
wood, pungent earth, and the fresh smell of alfalfa from a
neighbor's corral. I exhaled slowly and turned my head to greet the

beginning sunrise over the purple Manzano Mountains in the east. And then I saw him.

About ten feet away, he sat perfectly still, rigid and tall, staring upward to meet my eyes. The sun's first blush lit the underbellies of the clouds behind him, causing his faint shadow to spread out across the deck to touch my bare toes. We inspected each other a few moments. He was huge. Even in the dim light, it was easy to tell he was feral, his history of survival written in cliff notes across his massive body. A deep notch in his right ear left more air than ear above his head. And his stature, though proud, showed a prominent and boney ribcage. He had the biggest head of any cat I'd ever seen.

"Good morning and Happy Thanksgiving," I whispered, cautious of frightening him. He continued staring into my eyes, not a muscle moving. "I tend to expect an extra guest and you must be it. How about a little breakfast?" He sat statuesque, black as the night he came from. *Could he be deaf?*

"I'll get you a bite to eat, if you like?" No comment. His huge eyes stared, unblinking. I slowly backed up and turned the knob, watching him as he followed my quiet movements. His frozen and silent posture was eerie. I was hesitant to turn my back on him. What if he was rabid? What if he tried to run past me into the house? But immediately came a knowing that he was starving, yes; but rabid? No. I turned and went inside.

My cats, Deidre and Cochon, had awoken from their first nap of the day. Deidre jumped onto the deep adobe windowsill by the front door and, surprisingly, Cochon joined her. They heard me speaking and Deidre, being the good guard cat she was, had come to see who was out there.

"Okay, kids, we have company," I said, crossing the cool stone floor to the kitchen. Getting canned cat food from the fridge, putting it in an old, porcelain dish, I carried it to the door and stopped. "It's Thanksgiving, Deidre, and you can put that hair down, Missy." She ignored me, all thirteen pounds of her at full attention, every hair raised to its fullest length. She looked two times her already considerable size, ready for battle as she uttered a deep sustained growl.

She was a beautiful cat—huge, amber, intelligent eyes, a longhaired tabby with swirls of black, caramel, and grey. She was the older of the two and had adopted Cochon the moment he came to live with us. She was also the Alpha cat. This was *her* home... Cochon was her adopted son, and I was her human, and she would protect us to the death.

"Quit growling, Deidre. And yes, this guy looks feral and yes, he could be sick."

She glanced at me coolly as if to say, "Thank heavens you at least thought of the obvious," then quickly turned back to the outside intruder. Cochon merely sat beside her, alert and waiting, watching with his dark, somber eyes.

He was much smaller than Deidre, weighing in around six pounds, a longhair male the color of a light gray sky before rain. While at the office in Albuquerque three years ago, I'd stepped outside between meetings and heard faint, mewling sounds coming from a dumpster. A litter of kittens had been dropped inside and he was the only one to survive. I kept him in my office where he slept all day in a covered box, waking only to lick kitten food I'd gotten for him at the corner grocery store. He never made a sound.

Stopping by the vet on the way home, we got the good news that other than being almost starved, this seven- or eight-week-old male was fine. I wasn't so sure. "He hasn't meowed yet. No hiss, growl, purr... *nothing*," I said.

He got his kitten shots, was dewormed, then she gently felt around his throat, neck, head, and shoulders, listening again to various places with her stethoscope. "I don't feel or hear any obstructions, no unusual lung or breathing sounds. Maybe he cried so long his voice is hoarse. Give him time. Once this tiny guy heals up from whatever trauma he had, I bet he'll talk your head off," she said. But he never had.

He rode home in silence with me, tucked into the corner of an envelope box, draped by an old scarf. Deidre had already adopted me, and when I arrived at the house she immediately took over his care, teaching him proper grooming and table manners. But he was so afraid of his own hunger that he slept in the kitchen. Even with food in abundance, for the next few months I found him each morning asleep by his food bowl until the painful memory of hunger faded. He ate everything he was given. And then some.

Though names held great significance for me, I couldn't find his "Everyday Name." I told my best friend I had tried countless ideas, but none seemed to fit. Laughing, I told her the only one that seemed appropriate was "Pig."

She had lived among the Cajuns for many years and spoke a bit of French. "How about Cochon?" she offered one day. "It means 'pig' in French. And if you say it right—think 'koo' and 'shone' with the accent on the second syllable—it's much prettier than Pig." And thus he was named.

Perhaps due to his inauspicious beginnings and slight stature, he was shier and more cautious than Deidre. As soon as a visitor or animal approached our door, all six pounds of him disappeared. After they left I would find him hiding under some piece of furniture or in the back of a cupboard, protected from the strange sounds and presence of others. He was not a leader, not aggressive, but he followed well. In comparison to Deidre who swallowed the world she experienced, he just sniffed at it, content to watch from the wings. His nature was very loving toward she and I, but toward strangers, dogs, and other cats he was just plain wimpy. He could have been the poster child for the phrase "scaredy cat." It didn't help that he couldn't talk. Whatever happened before he was thrown away in that dumpster had either ruined his vocal cords or the sound had literally been scared right out of him.

So, when he hopped down and wanted to join me outside, I was completely surprised. "No, Cochon, not yet. Deidre's right—let's make sure he's not sick or dangerous first." Light as a feather, his small frame jumped gracefully back up onto the adobe windowsill and he continued staring down at the waiting stranger.

Dog-lovers tell me that dogs understand verbal commands, but cats don't because they lack the same level of intelligence. Yet I never lived with a cat that didn't understand their name and the words "no", "time to eat", or "brush time?" And then some, like Deidre and Cochon, understood darn near everything I said.

Opening the front door, I slipped outside quickly in case Deidre suddenly decided a face-to-face meeting was a good idea. The sun had broken the horizon, illuminating the stranger's shabby short coat. He was coal black from head to toe. Setting the bowl on the wooden deck a couple feet in front of him, I whispered, "Okay, big fella, have at it. If you like it, there's more where that came from." He watched me, intent and unblinking, following my every move, but he didn't budge. Quietly, I went back inside to find the two "kids" still sitting on the windowsill, mesmerized by the presence of this vagabond cat.

I returned to the kitchen to begin preparing sweet potatoes, and my mind drifted from the present back through reels of past Thanksgiving memories.

During 1986, my first full year in New Mexico, I was in unfamiliar territory called "The Land of Those Without Family, a Partner, or Single Friends." It made holidays challenging. My friends were couples with extended families who gravitated together for celebrations like magnets. Occasionally, I was invited in advance to join them. Most of the time, however, someone asked at the last minute, "What are you doing for Christmas?" or Easter or Thanksgiving or July 4th...

"I'm going to take a long drive, read, watch a good movie... and you?"

Ignoring my question, eyes would widen. "No plans? You're not going to spend the day *alone,* are you?" The anguished question came out with the same voice inflection as, "You're not going to have *all* your teeth pulled, are you?"

"I enjoy the quiet," I would respond, dreading the conversation to come. After a slight hesitation, the well-wisher would say something like, "Oh, I'd hate for you to be alone. We're all getting together. Why don't you come? We'd love to have you!"

These gestures were kind and well-meaning but felt like an afterthought. Words like 'perfunctory', 'cursory,' and 'addendum' came to mind. I thanked them and stayed home. Except for Thanksgiving, my favorite of holidays.

That first year I accepted an invitation for Thanksgiving dinner at my girlfriend and husband's sprawling straw bale home in Edgewood, a small community thirty minutes east of Albuquerque. As I was introduced to her relatives and friends, I felt both thankful to be included in such an intimate celebration and awkward in my role as fifth wheel. As the couples laughed and talked, pictures swirled through my head of past Thanksgiving dinners with my ex-husband and our friends, layered like a collage over deeper memories of the many imperfect celebrations with my own family when I was much younger. I remembered my mother, all-suffering, in the tiny, hot kitchen with perspiration running down her face and neck.

Mom hated to cook. It was a required and laborious task that came along with her co-titles of "Mom" and "Wife." She was an elementary school teacher with a Masters in English and a love of Chaucer. Secretly I wondered if she had missed her true calling in life and could have been a renowned 'Tanner of Hides.' There wasn't a steak, pork chop, hamburger, piece of liver, or bird of any kind that she couldn't magically transform into something akin to shoe leather. This talent was appropriate preparation for becoming a cobbler, but not for the future mysteries of fine dining.

With a will to cook the life out of any meat she put to fire, our Thanksgiving turkeys were dry, roasted over-long while she nervously opened and closed the oven door every few minutes. At first, it was to see if the bird needed basting. At the third hour, eagle eyes squinted, she searched the brown topography, looking for the red, plastic pop-up timer. Once it rose to full attention, just to be sure, the turkey suffered another thirty minutes because, after all, who could trust something plastic? Not until the bird had shrunk by a good quarter did she breathe a sigh of relief and banish thoughts of food poisoning and sick children draped over every couch with strategically placed buckets by their heads.

At bare minimum, preparing a meal requires good timing. But her turkey sat in the oven on "Warm," a word synonymous with "Dried Out," as she hurriedly made the gravy for the mashed potatoes ready in their serving bowl. At the dinner table, my baby brother elicited repeated admonitions to "Settle down!" as his excitement for the feast grew.

While Dad cut the turkey, Mom served the mashed potatoes. Plopped onto our plates in large mounds, a deft turn of her wrist pressed the serving spoon into the white hillock, creating a deep well to hold the heavy, rich gravy. We were experts at artfully maneuvering around the tiny pale lumps of flour floating in its golden deliciousness. Tired, home-canned green beans mixed with Campbell's Cream of Mushroom soup and topped with crunchy, greasy onions from a can were Midwest Mandatory. The whole banquet table was a sea of pallor, the only color coming from the bright red logs of jellied Ocean Spray Cranberry Sauce that decorated each end of the table.

But Mom's tour de force, the dish that elicited sighs of culinary anticipation, was her stuffing. Made with white bread she had cubed and dried for days in a huge, unreachable bowl on top of the refrigerator, she added boiling homemade stock, butter, onions, celery, eggs, poultry seasoning and extra hand-rubbed sage. Stuffing went into the turkey, around the turkey, and nestled into a separate pan in cute, little mounds. It could stop your heart it was so delicious.

Sometimes our family of seven would eat alone, sometimes with a cast of extras—a newly divorced and lost cohort of my dad's; an African exchange student from the university that babbled enthusiastically in broken English as we kids secretly rolled our eyes at every mispronunciation; or one of our friends that had temporarily run away from home, much preferring the relative sanity of our table to their own.

But the glue that bound us, that ineffable quality that made even dry turkey melt in your mouth, was that we were *family*. Though dysfunctional in myriad ways, though the love was flawed, the simple caring we had for each other mixed with our shared history, no matter how turbulent, engaged the heart; not only the senses. Love interlaced with years of repetition turned even the simplest experience into an event of intimacy and inclusion.

Now sitting amongst my girlfriend's family feasting at the table, I sorely missed my own and envied the closeness these people shared. My old sidekick, Sadness, joined Longing and Envy as a wave of self-pity the size of a tsunami washed over me. The familiar record began to play.

Other than my cats, hadn't I lost everything that mattered? A home, job, friends I loved, proximity to family, and the man I thought I had married for life were all gone. I became very busy pushing peas around on my plate so no one would see my eyes watering.

I have been here over and over, reliving the past, blaming him, blaming me, suffering until my physical heart hurts. I'm so sick and tired of feeling this way...

I had gotten used to feeling sorry for myself. But that day it felt dangerous. Dangerous because licking my wounds was *so* familiar; there was a sick kind of comfort in the quicksand pulling me down. My pity party began like it did on so many other occasions as I went over and over the past, yet couldn't stop, didn't want to stop, didn't know how to stop.

Lost in my despondency, I ignored the buoyant conversation around me until someone slammed their hand on the table. "And you know what he said?" It was Jerry, a big guy in his fifties who'd been telling a joke I was ignoring as I nursed my wounds. He was grinning ear to ear and leaning toward the group that was waiting with bated breath.

"What, Jerry? What!" demanded my girlfriend.

"Tell us the punchline! What'd he say?" squeaked Aunt Marge.

He paused, letting the suspense build. Then he said in a loud voice, "Well, it might'a stung, but it wasn't fatal!" and everyone roared. It must have been a great joke because people laughed so hard that some were gasping for air between fits of laughter.

Aunt Marge wiped her eyes and piped up, "Bless the widows and orphans, right?" And everyone roared again.

I never did hear what the joke was. But I heard the punchline, loud and clear. So clear that it felt like someone had spoken directly to me and Jerry had just been the messenger.

"It might'a stung, but it wasn't fatal."

It was one of those magical moments where the right thing was said at the right time and a life was changed. It was what I called a "kaleidoscope moment" —when the most infinitesimal turn creates a soft click as the tiny pieces reconfigure. Same content, different perception.

Click.

And my life changed. As I drove back home through the waning light of Tijeras Canyon, I wrapped the arms of my heart around the truth: I was stung, but it hadn't been fatal. The pain I had been feeling was a mixture of confusion and grief on the surface, and self-punishing guilt and rejection at its dark core. And in that moment, something shifted, and I saw I hadn't been rejected... I had been liberated. Liberated.

I savored the word in my mouth: "Liberated." I said it louder, "Liberated!" Then, I honked the horn and laughed and tears filled my eyes. I think they were tears of relief. And gratitude. I wasn't sure what I was thankful to or for exactly. But the change was so complete, it felt almost miraculous, like I had been bonked on the head with a magic wand held by some vast universal power. I leaned out the window as far as I could, wind whipping my hair, and yelled into the night, "I'm here! I'm okay!" Some coyotes in the dark canyon howled back, the perfect amen.

I was free, liberated from my own prison of self-pity.

For the first time in such a long time, I was deeply glad to be alive. I literally felt my presence in the world. I was here. All of me. It hadn't been fatal. I had just *acted* like it was.

The liberated are victims no more. As sure as I was of my next breath, I knew the drowning feeling of being a victim was over. As I rolled up the window and finished the drive home, I was in awe of how one simple sentence could change a perspective. Could change the course of a life.

Later that night, after feeding the cats and settling in bed, the other phrase I'd heard bubbled up from my memory: "Bless the widows and orphans." Where had I heard that before? Then I remembered.

Every childhood summer, we visited my grandparents in the foothills of the Appalachians. Because our trips were never long enough and they didn't want to miss a minute of being with us, they would forgo "sitting church" and stay home with us on Sundays. While the other kids played, I got to go visiting with Mamaw. She called this "working church" because, as she said, "You have to work a bit, not just sit on your hiney." So, off we would go in their beat-up Ford pickup to drop off items from her cupboards. One day, as she wrapped homemade canned peaches in a thin towel to put in the box, I asked, "Are they poor, Mamaw?"

"Just down on their luck a mite... widows and orphans, you know?" she said, rearranging the items.

"I know what that means." I was proud to show off my budding vocabulary. "Mom or dad or both died, right?"

"No, honey. Nobody died. It's just sometimes life gets mighty hard and we *feel* like widows or orphans." Then she sat down and pulled her little bible from the depths of her deep apron pocket that held so many surprises for an eight-year-old: a stick of Black Jack gum, a hard candy, an embroidered hanky, a paper clip, and evidently, the little book she opened. "Your mamaw doesn't have a lot of book learnin' like your mom and dad, but I pray and think about what it says." She squinted as she looked down at her small, worn bible. Then she read, "Religion clean and undefiled before God and the Father is this: to visit the orphans and widows in their distress." She closed it, and back it went into the depths of her flowered apron pocket. Then, she looked at me and said, "I figure if ever'body would understand just this one little line out of the Good Book, the heartbeat of the world would change."

I'd forgotten our conversation until that night as I lay in bed with Deidre and Cochon snuggled beside me. I thought a lot about that phrase and perhaps finally understood my grandmother's brief observation about the world's heartbeat. "Widows and orphans" wasn't only a literal description. It also referred to those who were lost, alone, disconnected, or unable to provide for themselves, even temporarily. Weren't we all widows and orphans at one time or another in our lives? I think she wanted my heart to beat with kindness.

I decided that next year I would find some of those "widows and orphans" to join me for Thanksgiving, no matter my circumstances. I refused to spend another holiday feeling sorry for myself. That door had closed. To this day, I'm thankful for the joke I never heard and the punchline I did.

3

Widows and Orphans Dinner

"The people who give you their food give you their heart."
– Cesar Chavez

During 1987, my second year in New Mexico, the NY Giants won the Superbowl, Robert Fulghum encouraged us to clean up our own mess, Steve Winwood reminded us of a higher love, and I remained unattached as another November loomed.

Before anyone could give that pitiful look and invite me to join them, I called everyone I knew and proclaimed the first "Widows and Orphans Thanksgiving Dinner." Did they know anyone with no place to go? I encouraged them to pass the word. The circumstances of the invitees didn't matter; my only thought was to fill my little apartment with people who would otherwise be alone. I figured I could feed four at the kitchen table and four around the coffee table.

People spread the word and that year I had four guests: a genteel, tattered, homeless man in his thirties, a newly divorced and bewildered law professor from the University of New Mexico, a PTSD-disabled war veteran who jumped at every loud sound, and a neighbor who sold Amway by day, waitressed by night, but still hadn't made enough money to fly home to Boston. Only two requests were made: call if they couldn't come and bring a container so they could take food home.

Unlike my anguished mother, I loved to cook and loved to serve. A restaurant owner once told me to never eat where the cook was angry; I'd get indigestion for sure. He believed the preparer's mood was powerful and seeped into everything.

I approached the dinner like a ballet of intricate steps, setting out utensils, pots, pans, bowls... measuring, cutting, chopping, mixing... baking, sautéing, wiping counters and stove, washing and putting things away... decorating and setting the table. The creation of the meal was the dance, and the background symphony was the pure delight felt as I prepared each dish. The simple gratitude and joy while creating this meal made the food mouth-watering, nourishing, and uplifting. It just made you feel good to eat it.

A year later, in 1988, I had six guests. One of the original four returned with two new guests and the other three came from an overflowing homeless shelter. Some sat at the table in the kitchen and some at the coffee table in the little living room.

Most were strangers never to be seen again as they continued through life. Some would arrive forlorn and shy, while others were loud, boisterous, and prepared to defend their circumstances. But no one was ever asked why they lived at the YMCA, or how they lost their job, or when they'd gotten divorced, or why their family didn't want them around. We all just ate and laughed and talked and ate some more.

Both years as we sat down to dinner, they expected me to say a prayer. They bowed their heads as eyes moved furtively for clues as to who would speak or what they should do. But repeating a prayer by rote didn't feel worthy of the moment.

"Instead of the usual prayer, I'd prefer to tell you what I'm grateful for. Anyone who would like to do the same, please join me. So..." and I paused, taking time to make eye contact with each person. I held my hands out to either side and felt hands slip into mine. "I'm grateful you came so I don't have to eat all alone on Thanksgiving." Everyone chuckled and reached out to also hold their neighbors' hands. "I want to say thank you for my life and all the many gifts I've received. I feel truly blessed. And last, I'm almost ecstatic for the opportunity you have given me to cook and serve my favorite meal!" I grinned. Keeping it light and simple was my internal rule. I squeezed the hands of my neighbors and waited.

An awkward silence ensued until someone finally spoke up. Usually, the first person to speak would also be simple and light, sometimes even comical.

"I'm thankful I brought the giant-sized Cool Whip container!"

Everyone laughed as someone muttered, "Never thought of Cool Whip. 'I Can't Believe It's Not Butter' is gonna be *way* too small." More chuckles.

Or "I'm grateful I'm hungry, 'cause this sure looks delicious!"

Another small pause, then it would begin... the homage to the simple gifts: a roof that didn't leak; an almost-new sleeping bag because it gets cold under the bridge; the companionship of a stray dog; the promise of work; a whole fresh cigarette never smoked by anyone else; laughter instead of tears; hope; a hug from a stranger; a good job; a new friend; still being able to see their kids; being clean and sober for 62 days; a new apartment; being alive. Though not necessary, they would include their thanks for being invited.

And then there was my favorite. His name was Nick and we met during the 1988 Widows and Orphans Dinner. He stood up, raised his glass of water, looked around at each of us and said, "I'm thankful for Dignity." His eyes twinkled at me as he continued, "Now, I know my being here is a gift to *you*, lady, because I'm doin' you a *huge* favor by keepin' you from bein' all by yourself." Everybody laughed. "Cheers to the hostess with the mostest!" Everyone raised their glass or coffee cup and called out, "Cheers to the cook!" or "To you, lady!" Then, his face became transparent and touched with emotion. "I came last year for your first do. I come back again because it was the first meal where I didn't feel like a stray beggin' for a handout. You treated me like a guest... ya know... wanted and all. Thank you for that, ma'am. I almost forgot what it felt like." He raised his glass again. "To Dignity!"

And everyone took another sip among murmurs of, "Amen, brother" and "You can say that again."

"Okay then," Nick continued, "Let's do this gal proud!" And everybody did. There was no conversation, just a background of soft voices and sighs and mumbled sounds of "Mmmm..." and "Oh, wow..." and "Could you pass that?" and "Oh, this gravy..." Sometimes the only sounds were forks touching plates, spoons scraping bowls, or a chair scooched a little on the tile floor. The comforting music of friends and home.

Though never asked to help clean up, everyone pitched in. Dishes were washed, dried, and put away, sometimes in places not found for days. The tablecloth and cloth napkins were taken outside to shake out the crumbs and then put into the laundry basket. Sometimes the floor got swept, sometimes not. But the containers brought by my guests left filled to the brim. Everyone who came was appreciative, and we hugged or shook hands as we parted. But mostly, they left me with a very full place inside that had nothing to do with my stomach. I hoped my guests had received something similar.

My memories about past Thanksgivings ended suddenly as a loud buzzing came from the timer, ending my reverie. I checked the turkey, then looked at the long table set for twelve. I thought how blessed I was this year to have room to spare. There were eleven confirmed, three from previous years.

With no more time for musing, I continued the dinner preparations and forgot the big, black cat with the huge head that had stopped for breakfast that morning. The kids, too, went about their morning rituals... napping, playing hide-and-seek, gazing out windows, grooming each other, and then napping some more, entwined so completely on the sofa that you couldn't tell where one began and the other ended.

It wasn't until the table was set that I decided to take a break and head out into the cool New Mexico sunshine. There was the bowl. The food was still in it. The feral cat was gone.

Our guests began arriving around two, and after countless hours of preparation over the previous two days, dinner was served at three and over in a scant hour. Bellies full, everyone still enjoyed pie and coffee by the crackling piñon wood in the kiva fireplace or donned jackets and took dessert outside to enjoy the waning warmth of the sun.

One sixteen-year-old girl named Annie, a name she had chosen in kindergarten after the class snickered at Annabelle, had a pronounced limp and couldn't walk without a cane. However, she'd brought a guitar. As others washed dishes and returned folding tables and chairs to the barn, Annie serenaded us after dinner with an eclectic mix of James Taylor, John Prine, Alison Krauss, and Billy Joel. Everybody joined in for "You've Got a Friend" and tapped their feet and sang the words to the chorus of "How Sweet It Is (To Be Loved by You)." The mood in the group was relaxed and upbeat.

Cochon had disappeared when the first guest slammed their car door and I knew I wouldn't see him again until the last one left. But Deidre was in her element and loved the attention. She wound her way several times through a group by the fireplace, sashaying around their calves, basking in the "Oh, isn't she pretty?" and "Come here, kitty." My cats had never been called "kitty," so she had to be introduced by name.

Some didn't know the proper way to introduce themselves to a cat and were disappointed when she pulled away from large hands reaching out to grab or pet her.

Most cats I've known enjoy a certain protocol regarding introductions. I call it the "One Finger Meet n' Greet." It starts with sticking one's pointer finger out for a thorough sniff. The cat may also want to sniff around the hand. If all is deemed good, the cat rubs its cheeks against the proffered digit, marking it with the scent glands on both sides of its face, letting the person know they are now accepted. This final okay signals adoration may begin.

Not everyone loves cats. One bald, surly guy named Mark, who spoke in short staccato sentences, said bluntly, "I don't like cats. They don't bark. They just sneak up on you real quiet like." He shook his head. "Can't trust 'em." He ignored Deidre's calling card of pheromones being placed on his pant leg and gently pushed her away with his foot. "They give me the creeps." Deidre wasn't offended and daintily walked over to another man named Peter who greeted her with a pointed finger. He was accepted and began stroking her velvet back.

"And *I* like them," Peter countered, "because they expect to be loved but don't demand it. And if it doesn't come from one joker," he chuckled, looking at Mark, "they move on to someone who *does* appreciate them. Isn't that as smart as smart can be?" He sighed. "Wished I'd learned that one earlier… I wouldn't have spent three years in the pit over my wife leaving me!" Nods and grins followed as Peter massaged her silky ears. "Like I said, they don't demand to be loved. You ever think of that? If you reject them, they aren't all hurt and pouty. See, Mark? Look at her. She's not even mad at you. She already forgot about the grumpy guy with the bad hairdo." Everyone snuck a glance at his bald head and grinned at the good-natured banter. Peter leaned back and patted his lap. Deidre jumped up lightly and began to knead his protruding belly. "They never hold onto past slights, which is more than I can say about us humans."

Mark shook his head. "Maybe not. But I still don't like 'em. A dog'll obey you. Just say, 'Sit!' and they do. You can control 'em. Cats? They do what they darn well please. And they're dumb— don't understand a thing you say. Plus, a dog *needs* you. A cat just uses you for what it can get. No loyalty there…" Mark muttered as he got up and left the group by the fireplace to refill his coffee cup.

Little Annie stretched her weak leg, then carefully set her guitar beside her, leaning it against the deep windowsill. "Oh, Mark, you're such a putz." Giggles of surprise rippled through the group. "You're confusing obedience with loyalty. Just because you can't boss a cat around you think they aren't loyal? That's a myth, Mr. Grumpy. Cats are basically no different than people when it comes to loyalty. People may not allow you to control them, but they can still be very loyal. And your comment about them not understanding commands? Totally untrue, by the way, because cats learn commands as well as dogs do if you spend time training them." She slowly stood, ready to limp to the stove for another cup of hot chocolate.

A woman named Cathy jumped up. "I'll get it for you. Sit down and I'll bring it over." She looked around at the clueless group and rolled her eyes.

As Annie sat back down, she said to Mark, "Edward R. Murrow once said that we must not confuse dissent with disloyalty." A few mouths dropped open, surprised at this young girl's discernment. I recalled her telling someone at dinner that she wanted to get her GED.

"Yeah, whoever that was..." Mark commented, looking around at the group, his eyes asking, "Who the hell's this Murrow guy?"

Deidre had gone to sleep on her back, legs splayed, head lolling against the crook of Peter's arm. He looked up at Mark. "News commentator, reporter, covered World War Two on radio and TV? He'd say, 'Good night and good luck' at the end of every broadcast. You might remember that," he added, gently smoothing Deidre's tawny and white belly.

Mark cleared his throat. "Oh, yeah. Him. Bet *he* didn't have a dumb cat."

Annie picked up her guitar again and started to strum a simple folk song. Everyone watched her curiously, waiting for another quirky but astute comment and she didn't disappoint. "Yes, Mark, and dogs are so smart it takes weeks to potty train them. Cats learn in seconds. Plop 'em in the litter box and they got it, ya know? They're quick studies, cats are," she said, strumming. "No matter what you say, you won't change my mind about these amazing little furballs." She grinned mischievously. "I think there's a song about that... 'I Shall Not Be Moved' by the great Mississippi John Hurt." She held us spellbound as her plaintive voice rang out clear as a bell on a stark winter night.

Out of the mouths of babes...

Time passed quickly. By 5pm, they were gone and twilight had settled on the land like a soft shawl. I'd been "picking the turkey" as my mom used to call it, removing the meat from the bones, separating dark and light into different containers, and throwing the skin away. I was putting the meaty bones in a pot to make stock for green chili turkey soup the next day when Deidre growled.

She and Cochon were once again on the window ledge, peering into the dark. I joined them. The stray was waiting.

I'd thought several times about that big old skinny cat throughout the day. A cat that thin wasn't eating what I'd offered either because it was too sick or it couldn't stomach the fare. I hoped it was the latter.

Because I didn't season meat, I could share it with the cats. I reached into both containers and scooped out enough turkey to fill the same old soup bowl, added some skin, and dribbled juice over the top.

Flicking the dim porchlight on and leaving my two mistrustful friends inside, I quietly stepped out and stood still, bowl in hand. He sat in the shadows, but the light bathed the front of his body and reflected off his eyes, so expressive in a cat. I could finally see their color—they were a startling copper, reflecting the porchlight like shining coins.

Unsure of his intentions, I moved slowly toward him, talking quietly. "Well, maybe you just don't like canned food," I said in a low voice, "so here's some *real* food. It's not raw and that's probably what you're used to, but hopefully it'll go down better than this morning's breakfast from a can." Setting it on the deck a couple feet from him, I backed up to the door and slipped inside to stand and watch at the window with the kids.

His head raised in micro jabs at the air, nostrils twitching. Eyeing the closed door, he slowly rose off his skinny haunches and slunk toward the bowl, hunkered and ready to bolt. A few more wary steps, then another, then a thorough sniffing commenced. A lick, a bigger taste and he began to eat. Slowly, his body halfway relaxed into a crouched position. He kept eating. Once in a while, his eyes would dart toward the door and he'd freeze. When nothing would happen, he would continue. He ate voraciously.

He reminded me of Cochon when he'd first arrived. He had eaten like this, hurriedly consuming huge bites without chewing, inhaling it before someone could take it away. Fear had driven his eating; fear of not enough.

I went back to clearing the kitchen, berating myself for putting so much food in his dish. No cat could eat it all in one sitting and now the leftover turkey would have to be thrown away. It couldn't stay outside to draw coons or coyotes to the house, and it couldn't be given to my cats in case he had something "catching." Returning to the window, Deidre and Cochon were looking in a different direction. Stretched out on his side he had moved to the edge of the deck, and was contentedly licking his huge paws, rubbing them over his tattered ears, first one then the other. The bowl was empty. "Well, I'll be... He ate it all..."

Suddenly tired, I leaned my forehead against the cold pane and sighed, feeling a strange mix of thankfulness tinged with sadness. I had watched my guests eat the same way that day. Strangely similar, they ate fast, heads down, eyes darting around to monitor their surroundings, their own fear of not having enough a familiar companion. I watched him lick his paw, then rub it over his raggedy right ear one more time. One more orphan had joined us this Thanksgiving Day.

"Might have a new friend here. What do you think?" I asked as I stretched out wearily on the couch. They ignored the question, intent on keeping track of his every move. A few minutes later, they both joined me, and I knew the big stray had wandered off into the night.

4

The Power of Words

*"Words have a magical power. They can either bring
the greatest happiness or the deepest despair."*
– Sigmund Freud

Normally rising before dawn, I awoke the next morning with a start, unused to sunlight streaming in the window. As I stretched and sighed, I found myself smiling. I loved these long holiday weekends. The world seemed to slow down.

Deidre meowed in a question mark from the floor by the bed as if to say, "Are you *finally* awake?" Throwing off the down comforter, I grabbed my robe and bent down to stroke her. "Love you too, beauty... good morning." She arched her silky back against my hand, leaned into my calf and rubbed the side of her face against it, marking me for the thousandth time.

So, the familiar morning rhythm began... turning up the thermostat as I walked through the hallway into the kitchen, pushing the brew button on the coffeemaker, calling out, "Time to eat!" as a mix of cat food and turkey from the fridge was put into separate bowls, then warmed in the microwave for a couple seconds to take off the chill. Snipped alfalfa sprouts were mixed into their food and the bowls were set before an eager Deidre. But Cochon wasn't there.

"Cochon!" I called and movement caught my eye at the front window. There he was, once more perched upright, staring outside. "Whatcha see?" I asked, joining him, caressing his slight form from head to the end of his tail in greeting.

The huge black cat was back, massive head turned toward the window, staring at us both. I quickly filled another bowl with leftover turkey, skin, and juice. Balancing coffee and food, I stepped outside to take a good look at our new acquaintance.

"Good morning," I whispered, setting down the bowl. I backed up slowly to the weathered bench by the front door and sat down. He gave me one piercing look, then stood up, moving cautiously toward the food. Wonder overcame me as I took stock of his size. I'd never seen a cat so tall or so long and with such a huge head. Even as emaciated as he was, he probably weighed a good sixteen pounds or more.

Inspecting him in the dazzling sunlight, other war wounds besides his deeply notched right ear became visible... fur missing in a crescent shape across his left cheek and another patch absent from his left rear haunch about the size of a quarter. On his right side, a narrow line of skin ran straight as an arrow from shoulder to ragged dew claw. The tip of his tail was bent, probably broken during some long-ago battle. He certainly wasn't handsome.

Leaning against the adobe wall, I listened to his cat sounds as I felt the warmth of the sun, a near daily gift in this land of enchantment. I so loved it here. The Manzano Mountains were blue-tinged and soft, slowly changing colors to the trumpeting bugle call of Sandhill Cranes flying in formation above. A Navajo friend of mine used to sing a song he called "Beauty All Around." It's a simple song, just repeating that same phrase "beauty all around" over and over in a melodic, chanting homage to the Great Creator's handiwork. I hummed it softly, witnessing the beauty in the cloudless blue sky, the pungent yellow Chamisa that bordered the property, and the buffalo grass that had turned tan with the change of seasons. A sweet feeling of peace filled my chest. There was a certain "rightness" about our guest's presence that pervaded the moment. He licked the bottom of the heavy bowl with great ceremony, then moved away a few feet and began washing up.

There was something proud and noble in this simple gesture. He was homeless, perhaps without friends, obviously with plenty of enemies, and looked like he was practically starving. Yet, he took time to bathe after he ate. You might think it's instinctual, this ritual, but I've met cats who didn't care if they were clean and groomed. They were sad, lost creatures, out of touch with their purpose, perhaps no different than a human in that sense.

We both started as Cochon thumped in staccato with his front pads. He was trying to scratch the windowpane but thumped instead with his foot pads. *Rat-a-tat-a-rat-a-tat.* His sudden change of behavior didn't make sense. Cochon wanting out was the antithesis of his deep-seated timidity. Since he had joined us, he had maintained a self-created ecosystem, and Deidre and I had supported his choice. This behavior was bizarre and totally outside his tightly controlled environment.

The big cat stared at Cochon's slight form, then at me. "Not yet, big fella, but if you become a regular and Mister Scaredy-Cat in there ever decides he wants to join the world, maybe I'll introduce you some day." I studied his movements, curious as to whom he was, his history, his motives. I set my cup down and leaned forward, elbows on knees. "Until then, I can't call you 'fella' forever, can I?"

Naming a cat is a decision of heft and weight. T.S. Elliot also believed names were important and meant something. In his poem, "The Naming of Cats," he said each cat should have three names. First there was the "Everyday Name" that was used to converse with it about such niceties as dinner choices, sleeping arrangements and other typical everyday conversations. This first name was simple, and you've probably heard common ones like Tabby, Kitty, or Fluffy.

The second name given to a cat was to be so singular and unique that it would be a rarity if any other cat ended up with that exact same name. It was a name that evoked such pride when spoken, that the cat automatically straightened its tail and puffed out its chest.

Elliot said there was also a third, secret name decided by the cat itself. It was not to be confessed to anyone else, cat or human.

Ever since I was little, I was fascinated by words. Each one seemed to have a power, eliciting a certain energy that included not only sounds, but pictures and feelings. Especially names. It seemed we could grow into our names—people as well as cats. A well-chosen name could echo our deepest nature, whispering of who we might become. This cat reminded me of someone.

As I sat, warming my hands on the coffee mug, I proceeded to tell our guest about seeing Michael Jordan play basketball on TV recently. Though not a big sports fan, I was fascinated by the power and strength in Jordan's 6'6 frame. I continued in a low, quiet voice, "He was very tall—like you—and so graceful when he jumped that he seemed to suspend in midair for a second. Kind of like Mikhail Baryshnikov, you know?" His copper eyes continued to stare at me. "It was magical to watch. And Jordan was literally feline in his suppleness. You, big old cat, may not be as handsome as Michael Jordan, but you have that same presence, that same energetic power and gracefulness. He's one of a kind. I think you are too."

Because he was so thin, his muscles rippled noticeably as he stood and put his rear up and head down, front paws stretched forward as far as they could reach. "You're a strong guy with a lot of power, no matter how scrawny you are or how many war wounds you have. Whatever you've been through, you've survived. That's more than luck, my friend. That makes you smart."

I thought of how people and animals grew into their names, how that name could bring a blessing to their lives, sculpting experiences as they matured. What blessing could I give this wild cat to aid in his survival? I loved the Spanish language and how musically it rolled off the tongue. The beautiful Spanish word, *sabio,* floated in the air. It meant "wise." I couldn't think of a better blessing for any of us, cat or human.

"So, for your full name, we'll call you Michael Sabio Jordan the 1st. It bespeaks grace and confidence in your prowess. It is the name of a leader who's intelligent and kind. I have a feeling you two have a lot in common. The announcer said Jordon almost chopped off his big toe when he was a kid, so you have that in common too, what with that tattered dew claw you've got. What do you think, cat? Do you want to be named after one of the most talented athletes in sports and blessed with wisdom to boot?"

The cat stopped licking and stared up at me for a moment and our eyes locked. "And, of course, we'll call you MJ for short. That can be your everyday, conversational name. The third, secret name is up to you, buddy." He continued looking into my eyes a few moments, then laid down on his side in the sun, exposing his belly. I took this simple act of vulnerability as his silent approval.

And so it was. MJ had come into our lives. Little did we know how long his strong spirit would be with us.

5

Still Place in the Storm

*"The least I can do is speak out for those
who cannot speak for themselves."*
– Jane Goodall

We didn't see MJ again until after our neighborhood welcomed in 1990 with a potluck at my neighbors', Gus and Emma's. On a late afternoon in January, an icy wind swept down over the Rockies into the southwest and the temperatures dipped below freezing.

Year round in the southwest, temperatures typically dropped an average of thirty degrees every night. With the ever-present low humidity, this made summer heat tolerable and the winters short and generally mild.

But this evening, the wind began blowing so hard that I jumped as a big tree limb cracked and fell off the cottonwood that bordered the drainage canal by my house. Irrigation ditches, called *acequias*, are man-made trenches that bleed off the Rio Grande, providing life-giving water to pastures and fields. Landowners depended on the unobstructed flow of these vital arteries for this thirsty area.

Squinting through the darkness outside, I could see the limb's black shape in the yard and knew at least it wouldn't have to be cleared out of the water's path in the spring. Thoughts of chain-saws were interrupted when the phone rang. It was my neighbor, Gus.

"I ain't heard one of these winds for a heckuva long time. Usually get these blowers in the spring, not winter. You okay over there?" Gus typically didn't say hello, just started talking like I was sitting right next to him at their old, worn kitchen table.

"I'm fine. The cats are in, but I'm not sure that barn will survive this wind." Dry snow pelted the windows of the house as the wind increased. The glittering white pellets under the porchlight swirled in confusion, tapping against the glass like hard sand.

"Nothin' you can do about that old barn. But if you lose power, you come on over with them cats and stay with Emma 'n me. We got that generator if we need it but the potbelly oughta' hold us. TV folks say it's gonna snow good n' hard too—more than a piddlin' couple inches." Winters were mostly dry, so his forecast surprised me. He paused in that polite way farm folk and Indians had in this area, giving me time to respond.

"I think we'll be okay, but I'll get the cat carrier out just in case. I've also got plenty of wood and I can—"

"No!" he uncharacteristically interrupted me. "You don't start no fire in that silly little kiva you got there! Wind's blowin' so hard it'll woosh down that chimney an' you'll catch yer house on fire. At the very least you'll be cleanin' up soot for a month a' Sundays." At that moment, his pride in the big, red pot-bellied stove standing in the corner of their living room was justified.

"Didn't think of that. Thanks, Gus, I'll be careful." Gus thought I was a real city slicker. And compared to him, he was right.

"Emma says she's makin' extra roast and berry pie just in case." He chuckled, his offer cloaked in pride, obviously enjoying the envy he knew I'd be feeling. No one cooked like Emma. No one. "An' I wanted to tell ya I seen that old beat-up black cat sittin' in your field a bit ago when I went out to check the chicken coop."

After they'd returned from spending the holiday with friends in Taos, I'd told them about our Thanksgiving guest. They both cautioned me about putting food outside. No one out here wanted to draw wild animals to their door.

I'd watched for him daily, even breaking the rule and putting food out once. Instead, a mother raccoon and her growing babies had eaten it before I remembered to get the bowl before bedtime. I chastised myself for putting it out. But MJ hadn't returned since that day after Thanksgiving. "I'll keep an eye out for him. Thanks for checking on me, Gus. You two stay warm."

We hung up and I walked immediately to the front door, opened it enough to stick my head out, closed my eyes against the stinging wind, and called, "MJ! MJ! Time to eat! MJaaaaaay!" My voice was lost in the howling of the bitter wind, the rush of tumbleweeds skittering across the deck, the needle-like snow stinging the adobe walls. Slamming the door, I turned the heat up a notch and headed for the family room. And as the three of us were snuggled together under a down comforter on the couch, watching the special weather report, we heard it. Somewhere between the wailing winds, a deep, long yowl rose into the night. MJ had returned.

All of us jumped off the couch. The family room had French doors at the south end that opened into an unheated greenhouse. On cold days like today, the French doors were wide open to prevent the various cactuses, flowering geraniums, and other plants from freezing. It was a perfect little warmth-catching room with brick floors to absorb the sunlight, full windows on two sides, and a windowed door on the end that opened onto the front deck. I went to the door and pressed my nose against the glass. Not seeing anything, I opened it and yelled through the screen door, "MJ! MJ, come back!" Then we saw him as he moved out of the shadows.

From his massive head to his hind feet, he was covered with a thin layer of snow. "MJ, come on. It's freezing. You can come in," I called as I held the screen door open a crack. He stood there, assessing the situation, then bounded over a small snowdrift and crawled under the furthest end of the wooden bench outside the front door. He looked up at me, squinting against the wind and yowled again. His voice was raspy, deep. "Hold on, I'll get you something to eat," I called, leaving the wood door open and the screen door latched. Snow began swirling through the screen onto the brick floor. "You guys tell him to stay," I called back to the cats as I sprinted for the kitchen.

Tearing pieces of a leftover roast into a bowl, pouring some cold juice on top, I ran back into the greenhouse. "Back up, you guys," the two guards were admonished as I opened the screen door slowly and stepped out into the snow in my slippers, quickly tucking the bowl under the long bench. Stepping back into the greenhouse, I shut the screen door and we all watched. He just sat there, head down against the blowing snow. "MJ, eat!" I called over the wind. Cold, feet wet, I backed up and shut the inside door. Immediately, he moved over to the food and began eating in great gulps. "Yes!" I called out, arms hugging myself with a combination of excitement and cold. And then an idea struck.

Carrying plants into the house, I set them on bookshelves, tables, and countertops. When the greenhouse was cleared, a heating pad was plugged into an outlet in the furthest corner under a small table, turned on low, and covered with old towels. A bowl of water and a bowl of dry food were placed near the blanketed heating pad ready for our wayward visitor. Then, like Hansel and Gretel, I left a trail of small bowls with roast beef—one just outside the door, another just inside, one halfway to the warming towels, and another one next to them. The cats were shooed into the family room and the French doors were closed so I could prop open the screen and inside doors with empty flowerpots. He had finished eating and was still crouched under the bench by the empty bowl. A strong wind gust covered him with a fresh skim of snow.

"MJ, come in. There's a still place in the storm right here. Come stay, my friend." Reaching down, I patted the cold, brick floor with my hand. "I'm going to leave the doors open and you can at least get out of the wind." He watched me. He knew what was being offered.

"I'm leaving now, and you won't be bothered," I said, backing away. Returning to the family room, I closed the French doors louder than was necessary so he could hear the sound. I sat back down on the couch and the kids stationed themselves by the glass panes of the French doors, peering into the shadowy greenhouse.

"We may have a guest tonight. Back up, why don't you, and don't scare him." They ignored me. I patted the sofa, "Come on, guys, back up and give him room to breathe." They didn't budge. Even though I've found cats can understand some human language, they are also incredibly self-determined.

The TV, though still on, held no interest as three pairs of eyes focused on the dim outside room. A few minutes passed, then an hour. No MJ. I fought the urge to get up and see if he was still under the bench, afraid that if he was working up the courage to enter, any movement might scare him away. After the ten o'clock news, the lamp and TV were turned off and we waited in the dark. The cats, weary of the novelty and not hearing anymore intruder sounds, settled onto the couch with me. Sleep overcame us.

When I awoke, it was almost 2am. The wind had quieted, and the snow had stopped. The clear skies held a waxing, gibbous moon that illuminated the snowy landscape and shone through the greenhouse glass, chasing shadows back into the night. Squinting, I inspected the dimly lit room beyond the French doors. And there he was.

He lay partially on the brick floor, partially on the heated towels, curled into a ball, nose tucked under his broken, skinny tail. The dry food was still full, but the bowls of roast used to lure him in from the storm looked empty.

Deidre muttered a small grunt from under the blanket as I moved to sit up. I felt for Cochon, both of them being "under-the-cover-cats", but he wasn't there. "Cush?" I whispered as my eyes searched the family room.

Movement caught my eye as his head turned to look at me. He was lying in shadow against the bottom of the closed French doors. How odd. Typically, Deidre was the one to "stand guard" while Cochon hid in the background. Yet, Deidre had deemed the situation non-threatening enough to disappear under a blanket. And he, the more cautious, timid one, lay in a relaxed position, separated by doors but still only a few feet from a strange, feral cat.

And the knowing came to me. He wasn't guarding MJ. He was keeping him company.

6

Use Me

"Love is a verb. And what's a verb, Old Man? An action word!"
– Emma Gustafson

When I awoke a couple hours later, Cochon had joined us, and MJ was gone. Something told me he wouldn't return, that he'd gotten out of the worst of the storm, filled his belly, and headed back to the world he knew.

I opened the French doors wide, letting heat back into the greenhouse. After sweeping the dry snow off the brick floor, I hurriedly shut and locked the outside doors, unplugged the heating pad, and tossed the towels into the washer. There wasn't a speck of dirt or a cat hair on them. MJ was not going to be domesticated. All I could hope for was to increase his quality of life.

Dawn was still three hours away, so the three of us crawled into bed and slept in the deep aftermath of the storm. I awoke to golden sunlight filtering through the bedroom curtains and the sound of a scraping shovel outside. The light was dazzling as I opened the front door to find seventy-four-year-old Gus shoveling my deck. The frigid air caught my breath and I coughed.

"Gus, what are you doing? You don't need to do that!" I said, wrapping my robe tighter against the piercing cold. He looked up, grinned, waved, and kept going.

I returned to the bedroom and quickly dressed, putting on two layers of socks. We didn't get much snow here over a winter, and we certainly didn't get this kind of cold very often. Zipping up my coat, I grabbed the shovel behind the front door and joined Gus, his red nose running, breath like smoke chugging in and out of those powerful lungs in that big, barrel chest of his. We worked in silence, clearing the deck, the walkway, and a path to the car.

There was something rich and peaceful about working side by side with this old farmer. People in the country had a different attitude about neighbors. Here, you depended on each other, helped each other out, stayed in contact. Here, you did for others, not charging for your time or expecting something in return. Here, you didn't offer, you just showed up.

I said as much to Emma later in the day as I joined them for afternoon dinner. We had already set the small table and were folding laundry together, waiting for the country ham to finish cooking. She stopped folding one of Gus's hankies, looked me straight in the eye and said, "Honey, that's Life. *Life* is about showing up."

But toward me, a single woman in her forties, they seemed especially attentive. As we shared the delicious, home-cooked meal that afternoon, I was startled to learn their only child had died almost forty years ago. I had assumed they were childless by choice and the revelation took me by complete surprise.

Emma was spooning green beans mixed with potatoes, onions, and bacon on my plate when she mused, "Our boy would be fifty-seven today." She said it in the same tone of voice as she would say, "Gonna get a bit of rain, looks like." I stopped, mouth open, and set down my fork, staring at them both.

Gus nodded. "Yup. I 'spect he woulda had grey hair like me by now," he replied between large bites of ham.

"I'm sorry," I said. "I, uh, I didn't know you had a son. I just thought you didn't want or couldn't have children. You didn't say anything about a son." I shifted on the old wooden chair, uncomfortable with their matter-of-fact declaration.

"Well, honey, don't you be sorry," Emma cooed as she reached over and patted my hand. "We don't talk about it much, so's how could you know? He weren't but seventeen, out sneak-drinkin' with his buddies. Tried to drive home and his truck hit a big tree on one of them curvy roads up in Corrales. It happened fast and the Good Lord took him right away." She shook her head slowly, smoothing the cloth napkin in her lap. "We told him to call us if he ever thought drinkin' was a good idea and we'd come get him, no questions asked. But you know young'uns... they're mighty independent and mighty smart." She smiled slowly, shaking her head again as she continued to smooth the cloth napkin in her lap, slowly, over and over, her gaze lost in the memory.

I said nothing, aware of the ticking of the cuckoo clock above the fridge, the soft scratch of her rough hands slowly ironing the flowered cotton square on her thighs.

"It hurt bad, mighty bad for a while, bad enough so's I thought I'd die. Kinda wanted to. Gus too, right, Old Man?"

She turned to him, and he nodded firmly as he buttered a piece of homemade bread. "Yup," he said, "We was durn near kilt by the sorrow." He went to take a bite of bread, looked at it like he didn't know quite what it was and set it on his plate. He sat back and looked down, studying his fingernails.

"He was our gift from Heaven, our boy was. After we'd been married a couple years, I finally went to the special ladies-only doctor in the city and told him we wanted a baby." She paused and I sensed she was weighing the memory against the words.

"Emma couldn't get pregnant." Gus looked up at me. "And it weren't for lack of tryin'. We'd been tryin' like all billy-hell since we was married."

A small smile crossed her lips. "The doctor did some tests and told me in no uncertain terms that I had female problems, too many cysts or something, and couldn't get pregnant and we should adopt. Well, we both cried off and on for a week and then started talkin' about all the little 'uns out there that needed a home." She chuckled. "A few weeks later my monthly didn't come, and a couple months later, the rabbit died. The next year Ronnie was born." Her face lit up as she turned to her husband. "We sent a picture to that smarty-pants doctor, didn't we, Old Man?"

Gus frowned as he picked up the bread again and spread raspberry jam on it. "Durn doctors act like fortunetellers. No good at it, don't know why they keep tryin'—tellin' folks they can't have babies or they're gonna' die 'a this or that or only got six months to live. Doc Parsons, who lives across town, says they's just practicin' somethin' called "defensive medicine." But I told him they was practicin' voodoo. Only folks *I* know wanna tell your future are them gypsy voodoo scoundrels. Pure shame to spend all that money and all them years learnin' and end up no better 'n a fortune-teller." But then he grinned and sighed, his eyes twinkling. "We showed *him!*"

Emma reached out and squeezed her husband's hand as she turned to me, continuing. "I couldn't have any more, so he was our one n' only. The sun an' moon just plain changed their course in the heavens and spun around our boy. We were so busy!" The sun broke out on her face. "There wasn't time for much of anything exceptin' Ronnie and his friends. Our lives changed. We stopped makin' new friends, spendin' time with neighbors, or payin' much attention to anything or anyone outside our little family." Her voice lingered over the word "family", almost savoring it.

"We doted on him, did everything together—school plays, hikes, church, vacations, sports, simple things like cookin' or readin' together. Gus and Ronnie worked in the fields side by side on the weekends and his Papa taught him everything about plantin', harvestin', tractors, keepin' the soil healthy, which critters to keep out of the fields and which to let in. And I was determined to be the best mama any boy ever had." She laughed, but her eyes were moist and shiny. "Oh, Lordy, the meals I made! Ronnie's friends loved comin' over here… any day there were fresh cookies, pies, hot bread out of the oven. Meals and treats fit for a king."

Gus bent toward me conspiratorially and nudged my elbow with his. "That's when Emma learned to cook real good," he said, lowering his voice to a stage whisper. "And thank God she did, because that woman burnt water when we was first married!" He laughed lightly, winking at his wife. She pursed her lips and chuckled, the sound tinkling in the stillness of the warm kitchen. His big, rough paw of a hand reached over and squeezed his wife's smaller but equally rough one. She squeezed back briefly and continued.

"We loved him somethin' mighty fierce. After he died, I never felt so alone in my entire life, even with Gus bein' right here. We grieved and grieved, mostly to ourselves. Just couldn't talk to each other or we'd both start cryin'. We were like two ghosts that couldn't see each other, walkin' around the house, cookin' meals, workin' in the garden, makin' the bed. We did things together, but we were miles apart." She shook her head. "We were a mess."

I hadn't buried a close loved one, but I had known many who had. Other than the hands of time that dressed the wounded heart, I'd been told it was the continued loving presence of the significant people in their lives that helped lift them out of the dark places. "But what about neighbors, friends, your family? Didn't it help to talk with them?" I asked, feeling momentarily desperate as I imagined them so separate and alone. "Widows and orphans" ran through my head.

"Oh, everyone 'showed up', like we were talkin' about. Brought food and come to sit a spell or help with chores. Deke Butler even put a new motor in the tractor and didn't want a dime for it. Said he was doing it as a thanks to Ronnie for helping him get through high school."

Gus smiled. "Had a rough time in school, Deke did. Ronnie wanted to help. They'd be out at the picnic table for hours goin' over school learnin'. Afore Ronnie stepped in, Deke were flunkin'. Never saw a boy work so hard, an' he passed with flyin' colors. Partly thanks to Ronnie, but mostly 'cause he applied himself and worked hard."

"He sure did," Emma nodded.

Gus studied the fraying cuff of his pale work shirt. "Deke's a good boy. Saw him up to the feed store yesterday. Had his grand-baby with him. Purtiest little girl, maybe four or five." He turned his attention toward me. "Deke were a little older than Ronnie, but they was best buddies," he added in explanation.

Emma turned back to me. "To answer your question, yes... people were kind, showed up to help out in all manner of ways for a few weeks, but then..." Her voice trailed off. She shifted in her chair. "For those who didn't lose someone, after a funeral life moves on. For those who did, life never moves on in the same way again."

Gus nodded his head and she continued. "After a while, nobody checked in much because we weren't close-like anymore. All relationships take nurturin' if they're gonna survive. We'd wrapped our world around our boy for seventeen years, shut out anything and anybody that would take even one moment from our time together... so people drifted away. We didn't even realize what we'd done, did we, Old Man?" she asked Gus, turning to him with a look of bewilderment flitting across her face.

Gus grunted, shaking his head. "Nope. We was kinda blind thataway."

"It's not that we didn't love 'em." She gestured out the window toward the other end of the snowy street. "I remember tellin' Ronnie, 'I just love those Sanchez's down the street. Fine neighbors,' which meant they helped if needed, just like we did for them. But when Ronnie came into our lives, we hardly saw 'em except to wave."

She got up to cut a few more thick slices of ham off the bone and brought them to the table, sliding them onto the platter. "Everybody figured out real quick that if Ronnie was home, we weren't available. People quit invitin' us to go places or do things because our boy came first. And wasn't he the whirlwind! There was somethin' goin' on or someplace to go most every day."

Gus nodded as he pushed his chair back a little from the table. "Yup. And it was 'bout a year or so later we was finally able to look at each other and see the misery we was carryin' around."

Emma bit her lower lip and winced at the memory. "It near broke my heart when I finally looked in Gus's eyes one night. It was after *What's My Line?*, remember?"

"Sure 'nough." Gus nodded, grunting a little as he reached for the coffee pot on the counter. "Sure miss that show. Steve Allen was a hoot. He could make anybody laugh, even two miserable, stingy old folks like us."

I was startled at their use of the word. "Stingy? How could you even call yourselves that? You're the most giving people I know."

Ignoring my question, Gus continued, "That night, we hugged and cried like two babies. Then we started talkin'. While we'd had 'im, we figured out we'd been purty stingy," he explained, stirring sugar into his coffee cup. He said it matter-of-factly, explanation complete.

Emma picked up a plate of sliced beefsteak tomatoes, red as blood, and handed it to me. "With love, sweetheart. He means we'd been stingy with our love, only givin' it to our boy. As if love was a well with a shallow bottom." She speared some green beans with her fork and then paused. "I got to thinkin' about it and decided that's pure wrong. Got to thinkin' on that word 'love.' I'd been seein' it as a noun, but it's not so much that. It's a verb." Then she asked me, "And what's a verb?" My mouth opened but I just stared at her, feeling like I was back in first grade and should know the answer. She turned to Gus. "And what's a verb, Old Man?"

"An action word!" he declared, smacking one big fist into his other open hand and nodding his head once, quick and short. I sensed they had had this conversation many times.

"That's pure right... an action word. Oh, we used to say we loved our church, our neighbors and family, our little town, but they were just words—all empty n' brittle like corn husks come winter. Love isn't about words. It's about demonstratin'. It's about doin'. I don't think feelin' love is one-tenth as powerful as doin' love.

"Doc Parsons says, 'Watch the demonstration.' He says the demonstration is the truth of a person, not their words. I thought on that and asked myself 'what am I demonstratin'?'" She guided the forkful of green beans to her mouth and chewed slowly, looking down at her plate but seeing something miles away.

"Then one night, as Gus and I lay awake in our separate worlds, I felt my heart beatin' too hard. It'd been doing that since Ronnie died and it scared me every time. This might sound crazy, but I closed my eyes and got real quiet. I didn't hear a voice or words, but when I asked a question, I heard an answer as sure as I breathe.

"I laid my hand on my chest. Then I asked this heart which seemed to want my attention so awful much, 'What do you want, heart?' I listened with all my might.

"And it answered, 'Use me.'

"Somethin' changed at that instant. I can't say what, except I felt a lightness I'd plum forgot existed. The first thing that came to mind was how I'd clung to what I didn't have since Ronnie died and had completely forgotten all I did have. Then I felt an explosion of pure gratefulness—for my body, my health, for Gus, this little farm, so many things. I didn't stop makin' that list for the longest time... guess I still haven't. And I saw that bein' thankful is love in action."

Then she smiled and leaned forward, speaking intensely but quietly. "And that's when the healin' started. We began to do. We took what we used to give our boy and started passin' it around, firstly to each other, then on to everybody else. And the more we did, the less we hurt. Nobody had to earn it or pay it back or say thank you. It was our turn to say thanks."

I didn't understand. They had lost their only child. "Thanks for...?"

"Look around you, honey! We are so blessed. Got these bodies to walk around in, a roof over our heads, clothes, air to breathe, water, food, a passel of interestin' things to do, and interestin' people to be with. Did we earn any of that? Not a bit. Life itself has loved us, pure and simple."

She leaned back. "Seems even two old fools can learn, and we learned that this here," she softly patted her chest, "is meant to be used. Love's demonstrations aren't somethin' to neglect or put conditions on or save for a rainy day. That kind of thinkin' was drying us up." Gus grunted in agreement, scooched his chair closer to the table again and asked if I could pass the tomatoes. Emma surveyed the table. "Better eat up, little girl, or we'll be eatin' ham and beans for a week."

We never talked about it again.

We'd all suffered losses, were all strays in a funny sort of way. But the thought that we couldn't save up love and dispense it only to the few or deserving, or only when we thought we'd get it in return, or only when convenient made sense to me... for people, cats, for all living things.

After that day I understood a little better why Gus and Emma were especially attentive. It wasn't because they were worried for this single woman living alone and surrounded by farmland. It was, as Emma put it, because there was no saving for a rainy day when it came to love. It was because love was a verb, an action word.

And without the verb, the noun couldn't exist.

7

Do No Harm

"Caretaking is different than care giving."
– Gary Zukav

Gus and Emma told me the winter of 1990 seemed colder than usual. After a couple frustrating incidents of trying to coax MJ into the greenhouse and failing, I gave up and fed him outside. He usually showed up in the evenings, called to us with that abysmal, ragged yowl, devoured any leftovers and disappeared. It didn't snow again more than an inch or so, but the temperatures dropped well below freezing many nights.

In the first week of February, another icy blast headed down from the north and we were promised our second night of subzero wind chills and low temperatures. So far, MJ had survived this unusual winter, but I began to worry where he would find shelter and even a little warmth in this kind of cold.

I wanted so badly to help him. I wanted him to be safe. But one part of me *didn't* want him to become dependent on me, something that could lead him to become soft in the hard world he had successfully navigated so far. I wondered if I'd crossed that Rubicon already.

The other part of me *did* want him to depend on me—to become a part feral, part housecat free to come and go with the confidence he had a dry bed, food, and friends. And tonight, those two parts of me were in conflict as I struggled to do the right thing and avoid doing the wrong one. I didn't want to harm him. I don't know when that became the primary tenet in my life, but it had been with me since I could remember: do no harm.

I thought of MJ as I watched Deidre and Cochon play hide-and-go seek with a box in the living room. Every cat I'd ever lived with was far more entertained with a cardboard box or paper grocery sack than any expensive toy. As I watched them play, suddenly a solution arose.

Working quickly, I sealed an empty box with duct tape, then cut a large hole in the front and a smaller hole in the back. In went the heating pad turned on "low" with old towels placed on top. I placed the makeshift shelter under the bench on the front deck, pulled the cord out the small hole in the back of the box, then ran it up the outside wall and in through the slightly cracked window by the front door. Last, I put a bowl of chicken scraps just inside the box entrance, hoping the weight of the bowl would keep it from blowing away.

Returning inside, I plugged the heater into a surge strip and prepared another bowl of food to lure MJ toward the makeshift shelter. The temperature was already in the twenties—would this be safe? The temperature would continue to drop, but what if the heating pad didn't cycle off and got so hot the towels caught fire?

These musings were interrupted by a hoarse, ragged call from MJ. Cochon ran to the door, leaving Deidre hiding in a paper bag on the kitchen floor.

"No, Cush, it's too cold." I patted the windowsill by the door and turned to him, hands on hips. "By the way, who *are* you? You don't act like the Cochon *I* know." He hopped back up onto the deep sill, and I patted his back, then zipped up my parka. "Wait here for me, okay?" Ignoring me, he looked down at MJ, and rubbed his forehead on the windowpane in greeting. MJ sat on the deck, looking back and forth from the window to the door to the box, tail flicking, nose twitching toward the scent of food. I eased myself outside, quietly shutting the door.

"Hey MJ," I murmured, setting a small bowl of leftover chicken mashed with zucchini down in front of him. Tentatively, I held out a finger toward his nose. He sniffed it, muttering something scratchy and low, and huddled down over the bowl. Returning inside, Cochon and I watched him gulp his meal, licking the old dish clean. MJ knew there was more and raised his head, nostrils still twitching as he eyed the box. Cautiously, he moved toward the scent of food. Stiff-legged, he took a step toward it, the hair raised along his spine. Another step and he lowered himself to face the opening, head thrust forward, then pulled quickly back. His tail was flicking wildly as he crouched low, ears turned forward to catch the slightest sound from this strange, brown cave.

It took him almost five minutes to move six inches, a testimony to his wary nature, and a trait that had surely saved his life many times. Then, head lowered, he crept toward the opening and slowly put his nose almost into the box. Another step and he lunged at the bowl, quickly dragging out a large piece of chicken onto the deck where he ate it in two huge gulps. Again, he entered the darkness and pulled out a small scrap of carrot, licked it, ignored it, and returned to the box. This time, he moved halfway into the box, and for a minute or so, the only thing visible was his skinny hind-quarters and a bony, broken tail sliding back and forth in ecstasy. Then, in one move, he disappeared inside.

The wind chill dropped way below zero that night. There was no snow, only bone-numbing cold and piercing wind. I don't know how long he stayed in his little cave, though I checked the box and the dubious heating pad almost hourly until around 3am. Feeling more assured each time that the house wasn't going to catch fire, I was overcome by a fitful sleep until the alarm sounded at six. I got up, started coffee, and went to the window, straining to see through the frost that covered the panes in lacey patterns.

My heart sank. The bowl that had been in the box was halfway across the deck, upside down. The heating pad cord was stretched taut, and the makeshift shelter was pulled out from under the bench. One of the old towels lay partway out of the box, frozen stiff and sparkling with frost. Something had happened. There had been a struggle, perhaps even violence in the few dark hours before dawn. I searched the landscape, but MJ was nowhere to be seen.

8

Walk in Beauty

"It is our honor to love you, not fix you."
– Hosteen Benally

In the first week of March, as I was putting seed in the birdfeeders out back, a faded brown truck pulled up and my friend, Jake, a proud Diné—or "Navajo" as most people would say—stepped out. Slamming the door, he held a wrinkled brown sack up high and yelled, "Yá'át'ééh! Grandmother's green chili sauce! You got anything to put under it?"

"Yah-ah-tay!" I called back. It left my tongue like music, as the peaceful greeting was carried on the breeze to my friend. I didn't speak Diné bizaad, the Navajo language, but loved the word that meant both "hello" and "all is good." It was recognition of the perfection of the moment. He joined me out back as I closed the seed bag. We laughed and hugged, glad to see each other.

Jake was a tall, lanky fellow who looked 25 though he was a good fifteen years older. Black hair down to his shoulders, he moved with a liquid grace I found fascinating to watch. Our conversations were intriguing, and I looked forward to them. I knew the feeling was mutual.

After teaching on the reservation for many years, he had returned to the University of New Mexico in Albuquerque, working toward his master's degree in education. He was a natural teacher. We'd met last summer at a class he'd given on 'Indigenous Plants of the Southwest,' and had been friends ever since. Before I'd moved to Bosque Farms, he continued to share his extensive knowledge of herbs and native plants during our long, leisurely walks along the Rio Grande. The overhead susurrus of the cottonwood canopy, and the species richness of birds, small mammals, and plants made these excursions magical.

Since I'd moved, he would show up unannounced every month or so, just in time for a meal. He could eat more than any one human I'd ever met. As we sat in the warm kitchen, savoring black bean enchiladas swimming in his grandma's green chili sauce, I noticed him looking at the birdfeeders through the glass of the back storm door. "What is it that calls you to feed the birds?" He gestured with his fork toward the structures hanging at the end of my clothesline.

"How many reasons do you want?" I grinned. "They're so peaceful to watch. Beautiful. Natural. Delightful." I looked over, watching the mourning doves eating the fallen seed off the frozen ground.

"So. You feed them for you, then, not for them." He nodded his head slowly as if he had received some great understanding. "I see." There was no hint of judgment, just an acceptance of my answer.

But I had been around him enough times that I should have realized Jake rarely made idle conversation. He truly wanted to understand my motivation. "Well, no, it's not just for me because they get to eat when the pickings are slim. What am I supposed to do? Let them die of starvation? This has been a bitter winter and they need the calories to survive." I was getting defensive when there was no call to be. I knew him well enough to know he wasn't judging me. "Maybe you're right. I do it for all of us—the birds *and* myself." I took a sip of the cold beer we had split into two glasses. "Do you feed the birds at your house?"

Jake typically chose his words carefully, thoughtfully. He believed, at a level even deeper than I did, that words have power. A few moments passed as he slowly chewed the last of his third helping of enchiladas. Almost ceremoniously, he carefully moved his plate away a few inches, turned sideways in his chair, leaned back against the wall and stretched his long legs out in front of himself.

"No, feeding the birds is not something I choose. Many disagree, but to me it feels like interfering. To interfere with a wild animal is to take responsibility for its life." Then he grinned, eyes twinkling. "It is enough of a challenge to be responsible for my own."

On the surface, Jake and I often seemed to differ in our views of life, yet we found similarities intertwined at a deeper level. "I respect that," I countered, "but for me... to not feed a wild creature when its life is threatened by this kind of weather, well, *that* feels irresponsible."

He nodded, considering my statement. "I understand. However, the strong birds know how to hunt food and survive, even in a bitter winter such as this. It is in their nature to know this. The weaker ones might not live through the winter because they aren't as quick or capable. But that's not a sad thing. They die and that weakness isn't passed on to new chicks. The birds that live are strong and will have the greatest chance of survival. They learn to endure. Everyone gets stronger this way."

He swallowed the last sip of his beer. "I've seen the goodness of your heart, so I know you don't want to hurt any living thing. Yet I wonder, when food is provided for them, does that simple act change their nature? I have to ask myself, do I want to change the nature of this wild animal? Am I wise enough to know the outcome of my own interference?" He shifted against the kitchen wall, inter-locked his fingers behind his head, and watched a small sparrow.

I leaned forward, both elbows on the table and nodded. "You're right, I strive to be harmless. And this internal battle of 'do nothing, do something' isn't new. I've wondered over the years if I've interfered in some way, but I value Life, so I keep looking after stray cats, try to save an abandoned nest of baby rabbits, feeding the birds. No matter how deeply I question myself, none of that feels bad or wrong to me."

He nodded slowly, understanding, absorbing my words. "You're right, it's *not* wrong. Or right, or a bad or good thing, but it *is* stepping in to alter a life's natural process. And once you've done that, are you always going to be here to feed the birds? You will leave this place one day and those birds that were made lazy by this bilagáana may not have the know-how or strength or tenacity to survive the next cold winter. And the next renters may not even like birds. They may keep a BB gun around to make sure there's no damn birds on their clothesline." He picked up his cold coffee and swallowed the last sip. "Grandmother and I just talked about this the other day, and she said it boils down to asking."

"Asking what?"

"Have they asked for your help? From what you tell me, that feral cat asked, showed up one day and waited on your deck. He wasn't asking for shelter or to be petted. He was hungry and something drew him to your door, and he asked for food. Because it was he who asked, not you who assumed, he drew strength from your gift. But that cold January night when you lured him into the heated box with food, he hadn't asked to be sheltered. In fact, he avoided going back into your greenhouse. But you thought you knew what he needed. Now you tell me something violent happened."

Earlier that afternoon, I'd shared the story of MJ, our Thanksgiving visitor, who had become a regular for dinner. I'd also told him about the box outside and the heating pad, the chaos in the morning and how I hadn't seen MJ for almost a month now. He had listened to the story without interrupting. Jake was a superlative listener. His whole body seemed to hear you and he never interrupted, and his whole being seemed to respond.

He continued, "As you tell the story of this cat, it sounds like it is possible you are drawn to fix his life because you believe you know what is best for him."

"Of course I know what's best for him," I said, surprised at his comment. "It's common sense. It was going to go below zero that night. What was best for him was to make sure he didn't freeze to death because I did nothing."

He smiled, then reached out and squeezed my hand briefly. "You said Gus thought he had been living feral for at least a decade. What has he done the last ten years when the nights froze, his stomach growled, or he got hurt? We don't know, but he survived all these years without trying to put his square peg body into a kind woman's round hole of a shelter.

"People are the same," he said in his low, soft voice. "They ask in many ways if they want or need something. Perhaps someone needs money and asks for it. You can give or not. But if they do not ask and you give them money anyway because you think you know what they need, then the act of giving can become harmful, even crippling."

He picked up both our cups, carrying them to the coffee pot. Filling them with fresh, hot piñon coffee, he set them gently on the table and sat back down. "Sometimes we don't question the motives behind our own generosity. Do you feed the birds because it makes you feel good about you? It is a worthy question. There is no right or wrong answer. If you are honest in your answer, it is how we learn the most about ourselves."

It was a good question. "I don't know. I think perhaps yes, sometimes I feel better about myself if I give." The faces from last Thanksgiving crossed my mind's eye. "But as far as being asked, sometimes animals and people aren't able to ask. They're too young, too sick, too old, or too hopeless. Sometimes they don't even know they *can* ask. So, you reach out to them."

Jake shifted slightly and his gaze was distant as he looked into the back yard again. "I know this truth. Once when I was gathering—a long time ago when I was still in high school—I found a frail, baby coyote that had either been abandoned or lost from its kind. He didn't ask to be saved. He shrunk away from me and hid his face, trying to be invisible. I took him home anyway, cleaned him up, fed him, and put him in a warm box by the fire. I chose to save his life if possible. I loved that tiny pup. I named him Bidziil; it means 'strength'. I hoped he would grow into his name. He was so weak..."

"What happened? Did he die?" I asked quietly.

He chuckled. "No, he lived and grew into his name. I wanted to keep him. I talked with grandfather about keeping him and all he said was, 'Love him enough to let *him* choose. It is not your choice. It is the little one's decision.'

"About eight months later, when he was able to hunt, I put him in the truck and drove back to where I'd found him. All during the ride, he laid his head in my lap and gazed up at me with adoration. I stroked his rough fur, sure he'd choose me over the wilds. We arrived and I set him on the ground. He sniffed the earth in circles a few times and then took off running into the trees, didn't even look back!" Jake laughed, shaking his head in disbelief. "It hurt my heart, but my pride was hurt even more. I thought I was pretty good company," he said, his eyes wide in mock surprise.

"I thought he had everything he needed: safety, food, exercise, a warm, dry home, and someone to love him." He took a sip of coffee and added a little more milk, stirring slowly. "I learned much later that sometimes baby coyotes are left up to a week by their parents. Instead of saving him, I may have abducted him. I felt terrible. At the very worst, my actions weakened him, habituating him to humans; at the very best, I was a waystation for his healing. I was too young and didn't have the wisdom to be respectful of his nature. Grandfather was right. He was of the wild and this decision wasn't up to me."

He paused, his dark eyes distant with the bittersweet memory. "Sometimes when I'm gathering plants, I see a coyote up on the ridge watching me and I wonder if it's him. I ask Mother Earth to look over him and thank her for keeping him well."

Suddenly, he stood up and stretched, then reached out and squeezed my shoulder gently. "When we love, that is the biggest temptation to resist." He picked up the dishes and walked to the sink.

"Which temptation is that?" I asked, getting up to close the back door.

"The temptation to change the nature of who someone really is into who we think they should be." He squeezed some lemony dish soap into the running water and turned to look at me. "I used to think that was love. Now I think it's more akin to anti-love." He rinsed a dish, placing it carefully in the drainer, and then moved to the table to get the empty coffee mugs.

"Bidziil was a wild coyote. I wanted to change him into a pet dog. But that was *my* desire, not his."

Then he stopped washing mugs and stared into the thick, luminescent suds. Slowly, he reached out his pointer finger and drew a large question mark in the snow-white carpet of bubbles. He gazed into the night outside the darkened window over the sink. "I wonder about intimate relationships. If everyone who 'fell in love,'" he said, sudsy fingers raised in quotation marks, "would just stop and look at the other person and see them for who they *really* are, would they reconsider? What if both lovers vowed to not expect the other to change or be different or grow?

"If they knew they would never try to fix or improve the other one, would they walk away?"

The idea wasn't new to me, but no one had ever asked me point blank.

Could I love someone exactly as they are without a whisper of desire to rearrange them in some way?

"It's a hard thing to ask of we humans," I answered. "To see the good in someone and not encourage that would be very difficult."

"True, yet isn't this what we were talking about in regard to the birds? You think you know what is right for the birds, but do you *really?* We're talking about birds and coyotes and people and cats here. Do we really know what is best for everything? How can we live in harmony with all things if we push and force life to shape itself to our desire? I suspect that birds become stronger when they learn to survive and are allowed to do that respectfully... without interference from do-gooders. Same with coyotes. I interfered enough to bring him back to health, and because I didn't know what was in his greatest good, I possibly harmed him even before I ever let him decide his course. And that feral cat. What is his name?"

"MJ," I answered.

"MJ. He asked for food. You responded. You neither added nor detracted from his life by feeding him. He would have found food eventually, being as resourceful as you say he is. But when you tried to domesticate him, he was no longer following his nature and you suspect he may have been hurt. Possibly, he now sees this place as dangerous and may never return." He pulled the sink stopper and let the water drain.

"But I've seen people *and* animals change when they're loved, and many become very different," I countered.

"I have too," he said. "In fact, I am a recipient of such love. But it wasn't because I was told that parts of me were wrong or bad and should be different. I wasn't manipulated by the promise of love and approval *if* I did what someone else decided was right and good. First, I was loved for who I was—warts and all, as you say." Jake grinned. He enjoyed my colloquialisms as much as I enjoyed his native language.

"Grandmother says people grow best in a climate of accept- ance," he added, rinsing a dish. "Even before I moved in with my grandparents, I was a real hell-raiser. I fought, smoked pot, stole things, and drank myself into a walking stupor. My parents divorced and Mom wanted to move to Montana to be with her sister. I didn't want to leave the Res, my home and friends. My grandparents offered to raise me, so I moved in with them.

"I changed because I was loved and respected for who I was inside—the *truth* of me, the core of me, not all the crazy exterior. They had the wisdom to see who I really was, and I changed over time. I think all living things change when they're loved in a respectful way. Their love gave me room to fall down, suffer, heal, and slowly discover what was to my advantage. They didn't tell me what was good, healthy, or in harmony; they let me discover it on my own. Because they loved me, they didn't fill me with their list of what I should do. They supported me. I became more of who I am, not more of who someone else thought I should be."

I shook my head slowly. "That's hard to believe that you decided you wanted to be this great guy and *bam!* here you are with your head on straight after leaving it lying around the Res for umpteen years. Seems they would have given you some advice, something more than just saying they loved you like you were and wouldn't judge you," I said. "Didn't they give you any guidelines?"

He grinned. "Yes, but very generalized ones, like be respectful, use good manners, take responsibility for my thoughts, words, and deeds. But they didn't pick on me or criticize me. They didn't say I had to change. They *did* hold me accountable for every decision I made. When they brought me home once after being in jail a couple nights, they didn't yell or punish. Grandfather simply said, 'All choices have consequences. It is our honor to love you. But we cannot fix you. That is yours and Great Spirit's job. If you choose not to live in beauty, your spirit and body will live in sickness.'"

I frowned. "What does that even *mean*, 'live in beauty'?" I asked.

He became quiet again as he weighed his words. "Your language has many words for our one word. In English you would say beauty, order, harmony, or balance." He smiled. "But then you'd need a hundred other words to describe in detail exactly what you meant."

"You're probably right about that." I smiled.

"Our word is 'Ho'zho''. To live in beauty isn't as much about surface beauty as it is the beauty found in the deeper essence of all things. It is beauty in the understanding that everything is connected and affects everything else. It is harmony in the physical, mental, and spiritual that results in a well-being of more than bodies." He paused. "Ho'zho' is found in the well-being of a river, a stalk of corn, a wolf, the air we breathe... it is all connected.

"My grandparents knew I must figure out how to realize this awareness and live it in my own life. There is no recipe; do this or that and now you walk in beauty. Instead, they offered me a living demonstration every day of what it was to walk in beauty. It formed their words and actions. Rather than talk of this thing, I was immersed in it."

He was silent again and I waited. Apologetically, he turned his hands over, palms up.

"I'm sorry, it is hard to define because my understanding grows with time and experience. Ho'zho' is living in harmony with the natural world. It is beauty, being in balance, sensing the order of things, feeling at peace. It is joy and laughter, respect, trust. Grandfather knew that in my physical and spiritual sickness I was out of balance."

Jake lightly placed the crusty enchilada dish in the sink and added more hot water and soap. "It took a ceremony, many days long. Family and extended family came to be part of it and help with building fires, cooking food. And in your words, bearing witness to the prayers and healing I was to receive. Grandfather hired a *hataalii* or 'singer' to perform the chant. I was struck by so many wanting such goodness for me. I was humbled that my grandparents, who have so little, materially found a way to do this. For me.

"It also took living in their presence to restore me to Ho'zho' so I could see I am connected to all of creation—people, rocks, trees, the stars... time itself. My behavior and understanding affects everything else. Knowing that feels..." He stopped talking and stood very still, staring out into the night.

I waited, listening to the ticking of the kitchen clock, the sound of the refrigerator cycling on. In a minute he smiled and finished washing the enchilada dish. "*Big*. It feels very big." He turned to look in my eyes. "I have no words that can describe it fully. Perhaps Ho'zho' is a love that comes from the awareness of belonging to life." He rinsed the dish, then the sink, and turned back to me as he dried his hands on a towel. "You asked a worthy question. That is the best I can do. I think it is something you must experience for yourself."

I began to wipe the counters. "I wish I'd known about these ideas before my husband and I married. It seems Ho'zho' embodies everything we've talked about—not thinking I know what's best for everyone, not trying to change them, seeking my own balance instead of expecting someone else to make me feel good. Aren't all of those really expressions of love? Had I known these things, I doubt I would have married him. I would have listened to my gut that pointed out huge disparities between his behavior and his words."

I hung up the dish towel. "I dismissed every red flag when I was dating my ex because his anger or his picking on me would show up, then poof! It would disappear and his charm and kindness would return. It only happened a few times while we were dating. But a couple months into the marriage he took off his dating persona, and the things I had only glimpsed became solid daily behaviors. I wanted it to work, so I did everything I could in order to keep him from being even more distrustful, critical, and distant. We tried talking, even counseling, but those ended in dismissal or arguments. I'd seen glimpses of the thoughtful, kind man he could be. I thought if I just loved him enough, he would change into who he really was." I paused.

Jake turned to face me, waiting for me to continue. "He never did. Almost as soon as we moved to Texas, he filed for divorce." I slowly shook my head, remembering. "The worst part is I had changed what I wanted and valued just so I could keep him from drifting away. I twisted into a pretzel to please him, pacify him, hopefully change him back into the person I knew was there. I ignored every instinct and swept myself under the rug... all to bring out his 'great potential.' I silenced myself. Eventually, I didn't even recognize myself anymore."

"How did that make you feel?" Jake placed his damp hand just above his waist in the middle. "Right here, in the core of you."

I stopped and thought a moment, trying to find the words to describe the sickness I felt after changing my behavior so drastically and still receiving a thousand small psychic cuts as I tried to appease him. "Disconnected... lost..."

Jake nodded as he dried a bowl. "Because you allowed your nature to be changed. Not by him, but by *you*. Maybe that seems harsh, but it was you, not him, who tried to replace the truth of how things really were with the fantasy of how you thought they should be." He put the bowl away. "And here we are, full circle, back to the birds, the cat, the coyote. People *and* wild creatures become disconnected and lost when they allow their nature to be changed. We put a lot of expectations on living things in the name of love."

Jake slowly slipped on his coat. "Grandfather once said that most of what people call their initial period of 'being in love' is more hormones and emotions than real love. He calls it 'peacocking': putting on our best face, best clothes, best manners, best self. It doesn't last longer than a few months because who can hold that mask up forever? I've thought a lot about this. I think he might be right."

As we hugged our goodbye, he kissed the top of my head and whispered, "Walk in beauty, my friend." It felt like a blessing.

After Jake left, I sat by a crackling fire and thought about MJ. I would continue to feed him when he asked, but I also knew my time of purposely trying to change his nature was over.

As I started for bed, Cochon came out of hiding and pranced to the window. I joined him, flicking on the porchlight to cast its amber glow into the black night. "Woo-hoo!" I yelled, startling Deidre who was snoozing in a box by the fireplace. Quickly filling a bowl with leftovers, I slipped outside and set it down. He yowled, raspy and low.

"MJ! I thought you'd gone forever. Come on, it's chicken, your favorite." I backed up, hugging myself against the cold night air. A small pain squeezed my heart as I realized he was limping as he crossed the deck. When he came into the full circle of the porchlight, I could see that his left shoulder was swollen and encrusted. A thin, pale liquid had run down his front left leg, matting the fur all the way to his foot. MJ was injured.

Was he attacked that night by another animal drawn to the lingering scent of food as he tried to find trust in a heated grocery box? Was this an unhealed infection from then or something new? Was my interference responsible for this?

I went back inside, quietly closing the door, and Cochon and I watched him inhale his meal, eating as if he hadn't touched food in days. The pain inside lessened as he finished and backed up to wash his face. I knew if a cat still bathed, it had a fighting chance. He glanced up once at us, turned, and limped off into the night shadows.

As I drifted off to sleep, Jake's words came back to me... "The temptation we have to change the nature of who someone really is into who we think they ought to be." Pictures began forming of loves lost, friendships long gone. Could a true act of love be more about letting go than holding on? What if two people could release the urge, the incessant need to change the other one? Could I ever incorporate this humbleness into my Life solidly enough to quit thinking I knew what was best for everyone and everything? Could I learn to respect and accept Life without the need to control it?

Pictures drifted through my mind – of the battered, black cat, the peaceful, grey mourning doves, the little coyote, and the faces of people who were gone, although once an integral part of my life. On one level, Jake and I had talked of the pros and cons of feeding wild animals. On a deeper level, we explored another brilliant facet of love. And in some magical way, MJ had been the messenger.

9

Touching Grass

"Tell me, what is it you plan to do
with your one wild and precious life?"
– Mary Oliver

MJ slowly healed, and by the end of March, he had become a part of our lives, showing up almost daily at sunrise or sunset to feast on leftovers. Deidre had become so used to his visits that she ignored his attention-demanding yowls. Cochon was the opposite. He would hop onto the windowsill, flicking his tail and rubbing his head against the panes of glass in greeting. Each time, I would stare at him in wonder and think, "Who *are* you?"

Though we had all accepted MJ's presence, I still felt unsure of what he might do if confronted by these two city-slicker cats. As I would head out the door with food, I would tell Cochon "No" in a firm voice, and he would glance at me with a sideways look and stay where he was. On the occasional day that MJ hadn't joined us by nightfall, I would find his small, grey form sitting on the sill, staring out into the black night, watching. Normally so timid and appre-hensive, afraid of everything and everybody, I couldn't understand this yearning, this fascination, this willingness to potentially put himself in harm's way. It was totally out of character.

One brilliant Saturday morning in the first week of April, I left the front door open as I walked onto the deck. MJ hadn't shown up for several days, which wasn't unusual for he kept his own schedule. Not seeing him, I decided it was time for the kids to finally get out of the house. I opened the door wide and called, "Want to go out? Time to greet the Spring—come on, you two!"

When we'd arrived last October, being outside for Deidre was natural and easy. Her hours were filled with exploring the big yard, chasing bugs, climbing trees, and sniffing everything as her nose identified her territory. I envied her prodigious smelling capability; her nose seemed to revel at being in nature.

But being outside for Cochon meant watching from his window perch. Eventually, if I stayed on the deck, he might slink out warily and settle beside me, his body filled with tension as he jumped at every sound. If Deidre disappeared or I left the deck, he would slink back inside. I would find him later, asleep in a closet or under the bed. So far, his feet had never touched the grass.

But today, he surprised me. Both cats followed me outside onto the deck, ecstatic with the smells of spring, the sounds of the world waking up, and the warm sun. They stretched and preened, rolling on their backs from one side to the other. Tucking my feet underneath me, I sat in the faded Adirondack chair. As I sipped my coffee, I closed my eyes, savoring the growing heat of the sun on my face and the small morning sounds that came from the Bosque... rustlings and chirpings, hushed and soft with the morning dew. Then Deidre growled. Instead of bolting into the house, Cochon joined her as they faced the eastern edge of the property.

In front of the house to the left, maybe twenty yards away, was the dilapidated barn. Gus and Emma told me that the original owners had used it over the years to shelter horses, dogs, chickens, and even a couple goats at one time. When they became too old to care for the property, the fifty-three-year-old adobe home, along with the barn and double lot, was sold to my landlords. The new owners lovingly restored the adobe to its original condition, inside and out. But the money had run out and the barn had been left to slowly decay. Now all it housed were folding banquet tables and chairs for large gatherings, covered in sheets of plastic. There was a small hole in the roof, easy access for the occasional rain and soft, grey pigeons during nesting season.

As the two cats sat frozen in high alert mode, I wondered, *Has an animal gotten into the barn?* The big, creaky double doors were blocked by thick tufts of tall grass, but the windowpane on the side window was long gone, inviting refuge for any animal able to jump onto the high sill and down into the sunlit scattered interior. As Deidre continued to growl, I thought of coyotes.

I suddenly remembered a conversation I'd had with my neighbors when we first moved to the country last October. At 8am, on the second day after my arrival, Gus and Emma knocked on the door to welcome me to Bosque Farms with a fresh pot of coffee and a pan of homemade breakfast burritos. I'd been unpacking boxes and hadn't eaten yet, and the aroma made my stomach growl. I introduced myself and told them about the cats. Before we ate, they wanted to meet them, so I quietly opened the door to my bedroom where Deidre and Cochon were cuddled on the bed, exhausted from the move. They quietly peeked in, I closed the door, and we returned to the dining table.

"Them's some purty cats," Gus said, reaching for a warm burrito as I set milk and sugar on the table. "That little grey 'un' would be just about a mouthful for an eagle. Gotta watch 'em while they're outside, ya' know. Hawks and eagles in the daytime kin carry off a tiny human baby, and those great owls at night'll crush a cat easy as a twig." He bit into the burrito, savoring the delicious combination of tortilla filled with eggs, cheese, salsa, and bacon.

"No need to scare her, Gus!" Emma admonished him as he chewed and grinned. She turned to me, apologetically. "It's rare to see it, but a Bald Eagle flies over occasionally, mostly in the day.

81

And there's plenty of Great Horned Owls that hunt by night. Both birds are mighty strong n' powerful. A big eagle can carry off a cat if they've a mind to, especially a little one like that pretty grey kitten in there."

"Oh, he's not a kitten," I laughed. "He's just small. He's over three years old, fully grown now. He must have been the runt of his litter."

She paused, dabbing at her mouth with a paper towel. "Don't you worry none. I think once your cats get some country smarts, they'll figure out how to protect themselves right fine."

Gus took a sip of his coffee. "Can't be too careful, Missy. Been a mangy old coyote (he pronounced it 'kye-yote') hangin' around that ol' barn a' yours. Better keep them dainty little cats inside. He'd make snacks outa 'em both, especially the runt." He chuckled, apparently finding the vision comical. I couldn't tell if he was teasing or not as pictures of crouching coyotes with razor-sharp teeth and circling birds with talons the size of meat hooks whirled through my head.

"Oh, hush, Old Man!" Emma told him. Then she turned toward me and offered, "Coyotes don't usually prowl around in the broad daylight, so just make sure your little-uns are in at night." She gave Gus a severe look.

He kept chuckling, then stood and patted his stomach. "Mighty good groceries, Mama," he said as he pecked her on the cheek. Then, he turned to me, gave my arm a squeeze and chuckled. "Welcome to the Bosque, little girl." Emma rose too, and they headed back home to the garden where the late green beans were ready for picking.

The memory of that conversation made me sit up straight and squint my eyes, searching the landscape in the direction of the barn. At first, I saw nothing. The fringe of tall grass around the barn seemed empty, but both cats raised their noses and sniffed the morning air. They either saw something I couldn't see or smelled an intruder.

I learned a cat's ability to smell is fourteen times stronger than a human's. I'd read they have almost 70 million scent-analyzing cells lining their noses, compared to our paltry 20 million. It makes them experience, define, and shape their world through scent. And though they're blind at birth for a couple weeks, they're aware of odors immediately, which is how they find their mother's milk. Add to that an extra smelling and sensing organ called a Jacobson's organ located on the upper roof of their mouths, and they are like smelling machines, aware of odors we would never notice. Combined with clear eyesight over a hundred feet away, they don't miss much. So, even though I could neither smell nor see anything, something was by the barn.

I stood, ready to shoo them inside, keeping my eyes on the tall grass. But from my higher vantage point, I relaxed when I saw a big, black head with a deeply notched right ear facing us. MJ was waiting, ready for breakfast, but aware I wasn't alone. *Should I leave and get his food?* Deidre's low-throated growl continued, growing in volume. She didn't look for fights but was fearless when it came to protecting her territory. She was also a couple pounds overweight, and her fighting prowess had yet to be tested. So far, her growling, occasional snarls, hissing and posturing had been enough to back off intruders. Would she and MJ attack each other if I went inside?

I didn't think so. After five months of feeding him, I'd gotten to know him a little bit. MJ wasn't mean by nature, just extremely cautious. His ability to trust was tempered by the world he lived in. It took him until a couple weeks ago to let me scrub the top of his head.

"Okay, you two... stay put!" I said as I dashed inside. It took only a few seconds to grab the already prepared bowl from the fridge and return to the tableau.

No one had moved, which surprised me. I figured Cochon would follow me inside, but he remained on the deck looking out at the tall grass.

Deidre was still growling, low and menacing. Then she did a strange thing. Lowering her growls to a bare minimum, she turned and slunk toward the front door. Just outside it, still voicing her disapproval, she looked one last time toward the barn, then walked inside and jumped up on the windowsill, staring out at the green field. She didn't seem afraid—disgruntled was a better word—and wasn't worried enough to stay. Stranger yet was that Cochon didn't follow her.

Surveying the situation, I thought, *Well, it's now or never.* I held the bowl up in the air and called, "MJ! Time to eat!" then plunked it on the deck, backed up, and sat down in the chair. For about a minute, he didn't move a muscle. Neither did Cochon. Then MJ took two slow steps, sat down again and looked at Cochon. *Well, I know how this is going to play out.* Cochon's history of timorous behavior, his unadventurous nature, would win out. Though he remained fascinated, I knew if MJ got any closer, Cochon would bolt through the front door and join Deidre on the sill.

As I watched these two size each other up, I was stunned as Cochon left the deck for the first time and stood in the yard. *His feet are on the grass! He's walking on the gol-darn grass!* My inner self jumped up and down, applauded, and ran in circles with a huge goofy grin on its face. But then my joy disappeared as Cochon jumped deeper into the bejeweled grass and pranced halfway through the yard toward MJ. It took every ounce of restraint to keep from yelling, "No!" and jumping up to grab him (even though the inner me decided to continue cheering.)

MJ gracefully walked through the tall grass to the edge of the mowed area of the yard. He meowed a hoarse greeting and waited. For a few moments, they stared at each other without blinking. Then Cochon simply turned and walked back to the deck and sat down by my feet, facing our guest. He had done his job. He had welcomed him.

When MJ finally reached his food bowl, almost five minutes had passed. Cochon had laid down beside me, paws straight out in front, making himself lower than the towering cat. And true to habit, after the last bite and snuffling the bottom of the bowl, MJ moved to the front of the deck, laid on his side and licked first one paw, then the other, washing his big, ugly head. Surprised, I watched as Cochon suddenly rolled onto *his* side and began licking his paws and washing his face, as if he'd just eaten. *Is he copying him?* I tensed again as MJ stood up and walked halfway toward Cochon, lay down on his side facing him, and closed his eyes. Cochon stood up and took two tentative steps, then laid down facing MJ, not three feet from his muscular, sprawling black body.

That morning, I spent an hour watching these two unlikely acquaintances make their introductions. One would curl a paw and then the other one would curl his paw. MJ would rub his face against the deck and then Cochon would do the same. They mirrored each other's movements, made small sounds, and seemed to doze for a while, acutely aware of each other's presence. Then, simultaneously, all four ears turned like satellite dishes toward the field and MJ suddenly sat up, glanced at Cochon, and sprinted off toward the ditch bank, disappearing in the tall grass.

That night, as Cochon lay curled on my lap, twitching occasionally in his cat dreams, I stroked his tiny body and wondered if this was even remotely possible. Could a mute, innocent, and painfully shy cat, who was afraid of everything except Deidre and me, become friends with a feral cat almost three times his weight and size? As they faced each other this morning, Cochon had looked pathetically small, the top of his head even with MJ's chest. And MJ was wild... would he turn on him one day? If he ever did, I knew he would kill him easily.

"I don't know, little one," I whispered, stroking his silken body. "The baby steps you took today were good. Let's take it a day at a time, okay?"

I didn't know it at the time, but this was the beginning of what I later came to call "Transformation Summer."

10

Transformation

"Love is the only alchemy that transforms people."
– Osho

Webster says that "to transform" means to change in composition or structure, in outward form or appearance, or in character or condition. But, as I tell this story, the word transformation seems inadequate to describe what happened that summer. A more explicit word for the experience was *transmutation*, a kind of mystical alchemy that turned base metal into gold, transforming not only a physical form, but a spirit into something greater than I thought possible.

Almost every morning since their initial meeting, MJ returned to eat and spend time with Cochon. As Deidre and I slowly relaxed into this new routine, Cochon became more and more animated and insistent, hopping out of bed in the early morning when he sensed MJ close by. It was uncanny how he seemed to know the big cat was coming. Even before MJ loped across the yard, Cochon would begin scratching at the front window. His nails found no purchase, so his foot pads would beat a staccato thumping that awakened me. If I was up but not in the living room, he would rub against my leg with an urgency that required stopping what I was doing to let him out.

After a few days, their greetings became more intimate as they touched noses, sniffed behinds, and circled each other until one or the other would fall on their side and stretch out, exposing their belly—that dependable sign of trust and contentment.

Cochon would prance outside, touch noses with MJ, then lie down and roll side to side, back and forth, his little body filled with a joy he couldn't express in any better way. While MJ ate breakfast, Cochon watched his every move. And when the big, black cat moved to a corner of the deck to wash his paws and face, Cochon would parrot him and do a little washing up too. They napped at the same times in different spots.

But since the first day they met, Cochon's feet had not touched the grass again. He reverted to not leaving the safe perimeter of the deck where he would gaze at the tall grass, long after MJ's skinny, bent tail had disappeared.

Then, in the third week, something changed.

It started innocently as MJ bolted off the deck to chase a dragonfly. He jumped amazingly high, showcasing his long, lithe body. I was reminded of Mikhail Baryshnikov, the extraordinary ballet dancer who appeared suspended in time at the apex of an exquisite leap. At the top of his almost five-foot jump, MJ caught his prey, turned a full 180 degrees in the most graceful mid-air pirouette I'd ever seen, and landed perfectly balanced on all four feet.

Then he turned to Cochon, dropped into a semi-crouch, and stared at him. When Cochon didn't move, MJ darted past him and disappeared around the corner of the house. Cochon waited in the quiet, a slight breeze ruffling his long grey fur, his eyes glued to the corner.

After a couple minutes, a small, historic decision was made. For only the second time in his life, Cochon stepped carefully off the deck into the dew-laden grass and sat down, waiting, eyes and ears turned toward MJ's exit path. More waiting. But no sign of MJ. Then, slowly and oh-so-carefully, he walked toward the corner. Suddenly, MJ bolted out from behind the side of the house, startled Cochon, and ran past him around the deck to the opposite corner and disappeared again.

Then, wonder of wonders, Cochon ran around the corner, and in a few seconds they *both* ran out from the other side of the house. Hide-and-go-seek had begun. They sped around the tan adobe a few more times, then finally gave themselves up to the energy that demanded release. I stood for many minutes, mouth open, eyes wide as my tiny cat acted like he was possessed by the spirits of warriors and dancers.

They ran, chased each other in circles, and flew on cat wings in a race to the back fence line that marked my neighbor's field. MJ won, but I wondered how long his record would hold. Cochon ran like the wind. They sprinted, they danced, they whirled like dervishes; they were tiny bug-catching rockets shot into the morning air. They were magnificent.

I knew Michael Jordan would have been proud. And I could not have been any prouder for Cochon who had transformed from "the little cat who was afraid" into "the little cat with the heart of a tiger."

They continued to chase and be chased until, exhausted, they plopped onto their sides, panting, eyes closed, ears like tiny satellites, turning in tandem toward the slightest sound. I watched them resting, stunned by what I had just witnessed, bewildered by Cochon's vigor and ability to maneuver.

He didn't learn these skills hiding under a towel in the cupboard. He didn't get that fast by running away to hide under the bed. It felt the same as if someone who hadn't exercised for years suddenly won a medal in gymnastics or the thirty-yard dash. He hadn't trained for this type of prowess, yet here he was, acting as if he'd slipped into a new dimension where he was strong and capable. Was this an inborn behavior, long dormant? Was it part of what Jake had called "our true nature"? Was Cochon's essence being liberated from the personality he had acquired over time?

I wondered if, in that garbage bin years ago, sheer self-preservation had taken over and dictated his choices from then on. Perhaps to soften the trauma, he had muted himself by staying unseen in the world. By staying silent. By staying small. A chill ran through me with the last thought. Could he have wished himself into smallness for so long that that he literally didn't grow?

Today, his body was still small, but his spirit had suddenly grown. As I watched, the thought arose that I was witnessing something I didn't think any person could explain. I didn't know how to make sense of what I was seeing, but I heard myself whisper, "Miracle," as goose bumps covered my arms.

After that day, I began going inside, leaving them to play with the admonition, "Stay in the yard, you two!" I checked on them every ten minutes to assuage my nervousness. They stayed. Slowly, I began to relax into the truth of Cochon's transformation.

When MJ left, Cochon would walk through the open front door, go to the water bowl, pass us without a glance and find his favorite sweet spot to nap. It was never in the closet or the back of a cupboard anymore. When I peeked in as he slept, he seemed to have a slight cat smile on his face as he dreamed. Cochon was changing. I realized I was too.

The woman who arrived in New Mexico almost five years ago, the one with the hidden soft center and hard, rigid corners, had been changed by the lands and its people who had reawakened her sense of wonder. Yet, living in Bosque Farms had added another dimension to my own transformation. It came from the people I'd met and shared my life with and the conversations we'd had that had been stimulated so many times by this feral cat. It felt like a long, drawn-out Christmas morning, a cascade of grace upon grace as each new understanding changed my shifting kaleidoscope of perceptions. Each experience awoke something inside that, like Cochon, had been sleeping.

This morning, as I watched this fearful, shy creature blossom before my eyes, I knew we were both blossoming. We had both received support. Though I understood so little of what this multi-faceted thing called love was, I knew enough to understand that support was one of its facets. As Jake said, it had happened without being judged or told we were doing anything wrong. Cochon and I were showered with demonstrations of what it was like to be loved for who we were. Whether it came from the people in my life or from a feral cat in Cochon's, we were being cared for—or, as my quiet friend had said, we were being loved in a respectful way.

The action word, *love*, had not been defined with words. It had been defined by MJ's behavior. Cochon had received a great gift. He received grace, something freely given without needing to be earned. I bore witness to the giving and the receiving of that gift. It made me a better person.

In May, I was outside weeding flowerbeds by the deck and saw MJ wander off toward the ditch bank. I kept weeding, not giving Cochon a thought because he usually went back inside to nap when MJ left. But this one morning, he jumped off the deck and pranced after MJ.

"Cochon! Stop!" I called in my sternest voice. He froze and sat down, his back to me. I walked over and squatted down by him, stroking his small, grey body. "I don't want you running off. Okay?" He looked up at me and then at MJ, who had also stopped and was facing us about twenty feet away. Continuing to stroke Cochon's head and back, I looked up at MJ. "He can stay with you in the yard, but he can't *leave* the yard, understand?" He stared at me, not blinking.

To cement the deal I picked Cochon up in a one-handed scoop, so light I never needed two hands, and held him firmly. MJ turned away, trotting over the lip of the ditch bank. As he disappeared, I felt Cochon's little body stiffen as he struggled slightly to jump down. "No, Cush. Maybe someday, but not now." I carried him into the house and set him down, shutting the door as I returned to the ever-present weeds.

As I continued digging up tiny rosettes of knapweed, prickly baby thistles, and the Bermuda grass that continually threatened to overcome my small patch of flowers, I thought about Cochon. Here I was again—do nothing, do something. Just when I thought I was done interfering with animals (and people), here I was doing it again.

Do I honor Cochon's natural instincts and let him trot off with a feral cat? Or do I simply do the job I accepted when I brought him home to live with us: keep him safe and healthy.

More questions surfaced.

Where does MJ go? Would he take off after something and leave Cochon behind? Would Cochon know how to get back home? Would he protect Cochon if danger threatened? If MJ got hurt, would Cochon come back here? If Cochon got hurt, how would I ever know?

Was I being too careful or not careful enough? Since Cochon was small and inexperienced, did that make me responsible to monitor his every move?

He'd had his shots and been neutered, so he was protected against diseases, rabies, and mating fights. But I couldn't protect him from physical harm from other critters. Almost every fiber within me wanted to let him be a cat. It was his nature to run, explore, play, and hunt. By nature, a cat is curious, territorial, and can travel long distances using scent to return home. I knew these things, but they brought me no solace. Cochon's purpose was being thwarted by my need to protect him.

But he was so small...

MJ towered above Cochon, whose small grey head just reached MJ's coal-black chest. When they played in the yard, it was like watching a grown cat play with a growing kitten. Yet, MJ exhibited a gentleness toward Cochon when they touched bodies and tumbled. More than once I had seen MJ jump sideways to keep from landing on Cochon's little body. He seemed to sense the smallness and fragility of his pint-sized companion.

He also seemed to know how to strengthen Cochon's budding self-confidence. In some ineffable way, MJ was aware of Cochon's need to explore his own strengths. MJ didn't slow down when being chased; he made Cochon run faster. He didn't just open up Cochon's world, he thrust him into it headlong. No kid gloves allowed.

A few days later, I watched as MJ went from a dead-on run to jumping halfway up the trunk of the cottonwood by the old barn. As MJ climbed higher, Cochon copied him and jumped low onto the trunk, sharp claws digging for purchase into the bark. He climbed a little way up the tree, looking back over his shoulder at the ground, five feet away. MJ ignored him, scooted down backwards, then gracefully pushed off, twisted midair, and landed in the grass. He bounded away without a look back.

Cochon stared after him, paralyzed. "You can do it, Cush!" I whispered as I stood by the mailbox. He appeared frozen, only his eyes moving as he looked up, down, and out toward MJ, then toward me. I quickly looked down at the mail, pretending I wasn't watching him out of the corner of my eye.

That's when it happened. Cochon made a small, faint, anxious meow. My ears strained, separating other sounds to focus on that one, tiny spot on the tree. I held my breath. *Did I really hear that?* He shifted position and meowed again, this time louder. A chill went through me as I took a deep breath, feeling instant wetness at the corner of my eyes.

Cochon spoke! He finally meowed—oh glory be to all there is! He has a voice!

Caught between wanting to jump up and down for joy, or run and save him, it took everything I had to not rush over, pat the tree trunk, and talk him down. Eyes still averted, I went over the junk mail studiously, acting nonchalant as I perused flyers for "Burgers! Buy One Get One Free!" and "10% Off! ALL Horse Feed!" After a minute, he scooted back down the tree trunk, holding on for dear life until he reached the ground. I swear he seemed to smile as he bounded across the yard to where MJ was waiting. I know I did. MJ bent down and licked the top of his head several times—a perfect cat accolade.

He didn't speak again for another couple weeks. Did he have to be in a dire situation to talk? That wouldn't happen indoors, so if the necessary ingredient was stress, I knew I might never hear him meow again. It didn't keep me from encouraging him at every opportunity, but he stayed silent, just looking at me with those big soft, grey eyes. It occurred to me that he had no need to talk inside because we anticipated his wants and filled in the spaces for him. Perhaps we weren't as loving as MJ who didn't cater to his weaknesses.

Silently I prayed he would remember how to talk and keep practicing. Deidre hadn't heard him. Somehow, I think she would have been glad to know he had found his voice too.

At the end of May, we were all outside enjoying a warm, almost summery day. I was raking last fall's dead leaves from under a forsythia bush as Deidre sunned herself on the deck. Cochon and MJ took turns playing their game of "Catch Me", alternately running around the house in circles and then resting in the shade by the oak. As I laid down the rake and stretched my back, I noticed Deidre had moved to the yard and was staring at the ditch bank by the cottonwood, MJ's usual place where he took his leave. "What do you see, sweetie? Did he leave?"

I walked over to the cottonwood, shading my eyes with my hand as I searched the higher branches for the two cats. Perhaps something had scared them and they'd run up the tree. But all was silent, not even a breeze stirring the tender green leaves. I called, "Cochon! MJ!" and walked to the lip of the irrigation ditch, looking down one long, meandering way to the right, then to the left, searching for what had gotten Deidre's attention. I searched the landscape of scrub trees and weeds, noting the small stream of water that moved lazily through the hollowed-out area. Other than the trickle of water, nothing moved.

Suddenly feeling nervous, I walked quickly to the back yard, hoping they'd stopped their ring-around-the-house chase in the back instead of the front. I circled the house three times, calling, looking under bushes and around the line of trees that separated our property from the back farmer's field. Nothing…

Nothing except immediate panic because I knew in my gut he'd finally done it and left the yard with MJ.

I stood on the deck, searching the landscape. That's when I noticed Deidre had jumped into the patio chair and curled up for a nap in the shade. "Aren't you worried?" My hand was shaking a little as I stroked her back. She wasn't, but I was.

I made myself sit down on the bench by the door and take a deep breath. Part of my mind screamed, "Find him! Get on your tennis shoes and get out there and find him! He's going to be carried away by some huge hawk! Or bitten by a snake and die a horrible death on the side of a ditch bank! MJ will save his own hide and leave him!"

I took more deep breaths and finally heard a voice within say quietly, "He's being a cat and living his nature. He is his own. Let him go." Reluctantly (and not without a good bit of gut wrenching) I did.

That day marked a significant change for all of us. While he was gone, I was frightened by my own academy award-winning horror movie where he ended up dead. Why didn't any of my internal movies ever see him living out a grand coming-of-age adventure? I admit I was relieved and teary-eyed when they both returned a couple hours later.

After meowing his greeting, which elicited a surprised stare from Deidre, Cochon accepted a few strokes from my grateful hand, then went inside to nap as MJ wandered off. Deidre followed Cochon inside and, like the armchair adventurer she had become, sniffed him thoroughly to see where he'd been. She licked his head and face before they fell asleep. I sat on the couch for a long time, watching them.

It was probably my imagination, but Cochon looked *bigger*, as if he'd grown a little since MJ had come into his life. Then I realized that thought had flitted through my mind off and on recently. He seemed a bit taller.

No. Ridiculous. Impossible.

Yet, I knew sometimes things happened before my eyes that daily exposure made undetectable. I'd had thirty years of cats as companions raised from infancy and I'd never seen a cat grow taller after the first twelve to eighteen months. They might gain a little weight after that, but a vet told me their bones usually stopped growing after a year. But Cochon somehow looked a little bit taller and stronger, and as he and Deidre lay together, he even seemed *longer*.

MJ was physically changing too. Though he didn't grow in size, his ribs weren't prominent anymore and his coat was glossy, a testimony to regular meals and possibly regular exercise with his friend.

They were both growing physically, but also in character. I knew I was anthropomorphizing, but I didn't know how else to make any sense of what I was seeing. They both seemed to glean comfort, confidence, and kindness from each other.

They were growing and transforming. And, strangely enough, I felt caught up in their changes and knew I was changing too.

11

A & A

"We need attention to survive and approval to thrive."
– Rhondell

By mid-June, a routine had been established. MJ would arrive for breakfast and Cochon would join him on the deck and wait patiently as MJ wolfed down his meals. Sometimes they left the yard and sometimes they just slept in the shade. Regardless, they spent the whole day together and their forays along the ditch banks became longer and longer until sometimes Cochon wouldn't return until sunset.

Another red-letter day was June 28th, the day Cochon didn't come home for dinner. Because there were few-to-no mosquitoes, I had become accustomed to leaving the front door open as I went about my business. I would stop what I was doing periodically and look for him, satisfied he was close by. If he was inside, he was already asleep with Deidre in their latest favorite chair by the fireplace. Then, I would check on MJ and most of the time he was already gone.

But this day, it was past sunset as I went to look for Cochon. He wasn't with Deidre, and she was gone too. *Oh, great... another one has decided to exercise their independence!* I stepped outside and found her on the deck, staring into the darkness. I sat outside with her for a long time until she wandered back in. Leaving the door open, I went back to doing dishes and working on a project I'd started. Around 10pm, I laid down on the couch to read with the door still cracked, my ears acutely aware of every sound. Waiting.

At 3am, I awoke with a start, spilling Deidre onto the carpet. I hurriedly checked his usual places to nap and called him. No Cochon. I went outside, and started saying his name into the night, trying not to awaken Gus and Emma next door. All I heard was the twittering of a small bird, rudely awakened by my desperate calls. I walked the perimeter of the yard with a flashlight, calling him in a soft voice. I ended at the side of the ditch bank where I shone the flashlight far into the black night and then went back in the house.

Finally closing the front door and locking it, I made my way to the greenhouse and propped open the doors with empty flower-pots. Sitting on the couch, I waited. I worried. I prayed for their safe return.

Movies of him stranded up a tree, or injured and bleeding in the dirt, or fighting for his life against a coyote, filled my head. MJ was a proven survivor, but Cochon was a city slicker with a wannabe heart. Part of me berated myself for letting him have this much freedom, for not taking care of him and keeping him inside. He was *my* responsibility and I'd let him down. He would be killed, and I would never know how or see him again.

The other part of me, remembering my conversation with Jake, allowed the fear to have its voice without judgment, knowing that beating myself up wouldn't give me any clarity as to what to do, if anything. But the part of me that pointed the inner finger won out and tears ran down my cheeks. As I sniffled, Deidre jumped up on my lap, looking into my eyes. One soft paw reached up and touched my chin. "Oh, Deidre, what have I done? Our little boy is gone," I cried as I hugged her. She touched my face again, then moved to the end of the couch and blinked at me. I laid down next to her and drifted off into a fitful sleep.

I awoke around 8am to bird song, sunlight filtering through the windows, and the sound of a cat yowling impatiently. Jumping up, I ran outside and there sat MJ, staring at me, obviously hungry. "Where's Cochon?" I demanded and then movement caught my eye as I saw grey fur bent over something in the driveway. "Cochon!" I yelled, tears welling in my eyes again. He turned and scampered lightly over to me, rubbing my legs, purring deeply.

Mute from birth, he had finally talked, and now he was purring! I picked him up, hugged him and he licked my face, struggling for release. I prepared all three breakfasts as Deidre and Cochon waited impatiently by their water bowl. Setting theirs down, I took MJ's breakfast to the deck. As he began to eat, I reached out and stroked him from head to tail and patted his side. "Thanks, big fella," I whispered, "for bringing my boy home." He paused and moved against my hand, not looking up, and resumed eating. It was the first time I'd touched his whole body. It was warm from the sun and incredibly muscular.

That wasn't the only time Cochon stayed out overnight, but it also didn't happen very often. Most of the time they wandered back into the yard together around dinnertime. A few times he surprised me by coming home without MJ, long before the sun went behind the trees.

One morning, a couple weeks later, Emma and I sipped coffee on the deck. She motioned toward MJ and Cochon as they played in the yard. "Those two have become fast friends. I think they were both lonesome."

"Cochon lonely? He has Deidre. And I'm no cat, but he has me too," I muttered.

"But you're *girls*," she said, smiling at Deidre sleeping soundly in another chair on the deck under the shade of the old bur oak. "Men—human or not—need the company of other men. He's got a 'runnin' buddy' as Gus calls it... someone to go do man things with. And my, hasn't he grown, your boy," she said, her eyes studying him. "He looks twice his size!" she added, squinting to catch the last of them as they disappeared behind the house. I stared at her, surprised that she was giving voice to what I'd only thought to myself.

"Emma, I looked it up in a book I got from the library. Their bones don't keep growing past a year and a half, except for a small group of big cat breeds. Cochon's going on four. But he *has* gotten bigger. That frail little runt disappeared someplace. I don't get it... maybe all the exercise is filling out his muscles?"

Emma sipped her hot coffee. "No, he's taller," she said emphatically. "I don't care what your fancy book says. He's not that tiny little thing we met last fall." In the middle of a sip of coffee, she leaned back in surprise. "And when in the world did he start talkin'?" she asked as Cochon meowed loudly at MJ who was now hiding under a bush. Emma grinned like a proud grandmother. "My oh my, talkin' and growin' to beat the band! I bet it's cause he's got a big ol' dose of A&A, as Doc Parsons calls it. That Doc is so clever and has the best way of sayin' things," she added.

"A and A? What's that?"

She leaned over and caressed Deidre's soft side as she slept. "Attention and approval," Emma said, grinning. "He says we need attention to survive and approval to thrive. Not just people, but animals too."

I immediately felt a little defensive. "Really. Well, Cochon gets plenty of this A&A stuff right here at home. You know I adore him."

"Oh, of *course* you do, honey! And after I'm gone, if that reincarnation business is true, I hope to heavens I come back as *your* cat. But see, a cat gets something different from his own kind, somethin' we humans can't give it."

"What about Deidre? She loves him like a son. She waits on him, grooms him, plays and cuddles with him, lets him have her food and favorite toys. She's his own kind and she literally dotes on him. He gets plenty of attention and approval from her."

"Yes," Emma nodded in agreement, "she does those things, but like I said, she's a girl. Plus, that's inside," and she hitched her thumb backward toward the open front door. "And Cochon lives two lives now: one inside and one outside, and both make him strong. He loves you both and comes home. But he also loves the wilds, and he loves his new friend. And you've allowed him to be himself." She looked at me. "Which I'm thinkin' wasn't very easy for you."

I chuckled quietly. "We had a few sleepless nights and a few tears the first couple times he stayed out all night," I admitted. "And sometimes," I whispered, "I'm so afraid a morning will come, and he won't come home. Ever again." Emma reached over and patted my knee. Suddenly, I was embarrassed, remembering her son that never came home that one rainy night forty years ago. I felt the heat climbing up under my collar into my face. "I'm sorry, Emma, I wasn't thinking. You've suffered so much more than I ever could. Losing a cat and losing a human are very, very different."

"You can't measure sufferin' based on the who, what, why, or when, honey. And you can't say the love we give to animals is less important or smaller than the love we give to people. You've let him go and that's what matters. You didn't stunt his cat growth by keepin' him in and mollycoddlin' his fears. That was no small gift you gave that little guy. You know how I know? Lookee there." She nodded toward the barn where the cats were playing hide and seek halfway up the trunk of the elm tree. They both jumped off and trotted toward the deck.

I watched their approach and Emma was right. No longer did Cochon look like a growing kitten. He moved with confidence and strength beside the panther-like body of MJ. And amazing though it seemed, the top of his head now reached MJ's chin. Emma saw it too. "My, he *has* grown! And isn't he grand?" As we sat and watched them stretch out on the grass to rest, Emma shook her head. "It *is* kinda amazin', isn't it? It's like a... a little miracle," she said softly as she watched them.

She turned to me. "What a glorious testimony to so many things... bein' loved, bein' accepted just as you are, attention, approval, livin' your very nature and purpose. He's a *real* cat now," she said. "It's almost like he was a little ghost of himself before." She squinted her eyes as she watched MJ get up and move to a different spot. "And that old stray looks better too—stronger and shinier. Though he's still butt ugly." We both laughed, hugged, and life was good.

I had shopping to do, so after she left I shooed Deidre and Cochon inside as MJ stretched out on the deck in the shade to sleep. As I drove to Smith's grocery store, I kept playing the scene over and over of MJ walking next to Cochon, how tall he had become and how confident he looked. MJ had become not only his friend, but his mentor, his teacher, his guide.

Can cats love? I don't know. But if they feel love or something like it, MJ loved Cochon in his own cat way. He encouraged him to do more but didn't reject him when he didn't. MJ nudged and pushed him—in the kindest way—to test his own strengths. Cochon's self-imposed boundaries were melting away.

Could it be possible that MJ's acceptance and inclusion, his encouragement and pushing had woken up some genetic force within Cochon? Could it be that because he didn't see himself as helpless and small, his new-found confidence had unlocked something in his very DNA that allowed him to grow? I didn't know. I doubted there was a scientific explanation for anything that was happening.

I ruminated on Emma's comments about being loved and accepted just as he is. MJ seemed to have done a much better job at that than Deidre and I. He saw him as he was, accepted him without critique, but made room for him to be so much more.

On the other hand, Deidre and I had also loved him without critique, but had reinforced his fear. How many times had I waited to open the door until I was sure Cochon was in one of his hidey-holes? How many times did I avoid taking someone into the back office if I knew he had crawled into the desk drawer to hide? When did I give up encouraging him to come outside with us? Ages ago. We had narrowed his world. MJ had opened it.

I recalled Jake's and my conversation about the same thing: people, coyotes, cats and birds. Let them go, love them like they are, accept them without the need to fix or change them, and always... encourage their strengths.

All I knew for sure was that I was witnessing something so rare, so inexplicable, that Emma's chosen word was strikingly accurate. To watch a three-and-a-half-year-old cat gain height, not just weight, and to listen to him meow and purr after a life of total silence, qualified as a miracle.

12

Doc Parsons

"The meeting of two personalities is like the contact of two chemical substances; if there is any reaction, both are transformed."
– C. G. Jung

I had heard of Doc Parsons from several people in Bosque Farms, not just Gus and Emma. Everyone loved him. From what they said, he looked, walked, and acted like he was in his sixties, but the birthdate on his driver's license said he was 81.

He had been a General Practitioner in our little town for around 35 years. Stories said he had been married to one Rosalie Benson and had a son and daughter who both lived out East. Rosalie had died of cancer about 20 years ago and Doc had stayed and kept working, making house calls, as well as tending to sick grownups and children for everything from heart attacks to measles.

He turned no one away and filed no insurance. He had a coffee can system. Whatever people could afford was put in a Folgers can on the reception desk out front. It had a 3x5 card taped to it that simply said, "Thanks for the Privilege of Serving You!" No one's offerings were ever scrutinized, and when a patient didn't have anything for the coffee can, Doc was paid in eggs, vegetables from the garden, venison, a few steaks from a local cow that was butchered, or homemade bread. Some paid cash and paid well. But he never asked about money and wouldn't talk about it. "Go talk to Lois—she'll fix you right up," he'd say to anyone who was worried about the paying end of the equation.

Lois was his office manager who came in the first day he put out his shingle. Her twin boys had poison ivy. When she asked Doc if she could work out her fee by tidying up the office, he asked if she could answer the phone, type, file, and if she was usually in a good mood. Lois told him she could do all that and if he hired her, her mood would be a whole lot better. He hired her on the spot. She never left his side and only retired when Doc did, thirty-five years later.

A few years after Rosalie died, Doc's older brother, Jim, who'd never married, moved in with him. The brothers figured why keep up two households when they got along just fine. Jim was a veterinarian, so the area was well served with the Parson brothers tending the sick, whether two-legged or four-legged.

Stories say that when Jim was called in the middle of the night to see about a mare having trouble foaling, Doc frequently went right along with him. In fact, he went with Jim so often to see about cattle, horses, goats, sheep, chickens, dogs, cats, and rabbits, that when Jim was laid low by the occasional bug, Doc made his house calls for him.

Jim, on the other hand, liked animals far better than people, so he never returned the favor.

Doc finally retired five years ago from his practice. A young fellow named Carl Beaumont from California bought it, seemingly taking Doc out of the picture for broken bones and strep throat. But because Dr. Beaumont lived in Albuquerque, only worked Monday, Wednesday, and Friday, and left the office promptly by six, Doc was still called at midnight when some kid had a fever or a couple of bar-brawl rowdies needed stitching up. Though retired, he renewed his medical license and insurance yearly. Dr. Beaumont was happy about the arrangement, though I heard Doc refused to sign a contract, saying instead he'd be around to help as long as he was able. It was a gentlemen's agreement.

Doc's brother, Jim, died three years ago. He bequeathed Doc his vet paraphernalia and a well-stocked pharmacy. The little town hadn't replaced its veterinarian yet, so people still called Doc for a goat with mastitis or chickens that wouldn't lay. He told someone he'd be available for animals until a new vet arrived, but so far none had.

He still wouldn't take any money. "I'm not a vet so let's just say I'm here to make a little contribution to the situation, okay?" he'd tell a worried animal owner reaching for his wallet. But he still received gifts: fresh asparagus in the spring or a big sack of pecans from someone's orchard. Fresh fish, venison, beef, mutton, or chicken would show up, well-packed under ice in beat-up Styrofoam coolers by his front door. His lawn got mowed, his trees trimmed. He didn't want for fresh eggs. And whenever he made house calls on the Isleta Reservation, the heady aroma of fresh tortillas or hot bread from a horno oven filled his car as he drove the five miles back home.

What people commented on most was Doc Parson's personality. Adjectives included, "smart, steady, kind, unusual, wise, patient, a character, and quirky." I heard that from people about their own doctoring as well as about their animals. Everyone still called him just "Doc" and they loved him.

On a morning in July, when Cochon came home at dawn, but wouldn't come inside the house, Deidre and I joined him outside. With the sun still pushing up behind the Manzano Mountains, he pranced away from us toward the tall, wet grass by the barn. Deidre lightly jumped up onto a deck chair and watched. I looked around for MJ in the morning shadows as I walked to where Cochon sat. As I neared him, I saw a dark shape in the grass.

Before I could say anything, MJ softly yowled in a ragged, breathy voice as he tried to lift his head. The sun broke through a cloud, and I saw blood matting the fur near his shoulder. "Oh no, MJ!" I cried, dropping to my knees beside him. I could immediately see he was badly hurt. "Hold on, boy, I'll get help!" I told him. "You're going to be okay, now... just stay put." A dumb thing to say as I could tell he didn't have the strength to move. He'd no doubt used up what little he had just to get back here.

I started to grab Cochon to take him inside, but instead I reached out and picked him up. He'd gotten so much heavier that it took two hands. "Hey, buddy, you okay?" Quickly I felt all over his body for wetness or bumps or places he'd react to when touched. I squeezed and prodded but felt nothing. I put him back down. MJ needed his friend's presence right now. "Okay, stay put, Cochon, and I'll be right back." He turned back to MJ and sat all the way down, just an inch from his friend's head.

I glanced at the clock as I ran back inside and grabbed the phone, Deidre at my heels. Almost 6am. Would this doctor everyone bragged about even hear it ring? Jeez, he was over eighty. Would he hang up on me for being so rude as to wake him? Was it too early?

He answered on the first ring.

"Mornin'!" a strong voice called out. "Animal or human?"

He caught me by surprise, so I hesitated a second then blurted out, "Animal. Cat. Feral."

"Okay then, what's your address?" I told him and he chuckled. "Oh, you're the one with the two city cats and the big, black stray. Gus and Miss Emma told me about y'all. Give me ten minutes and I'll be right over. Tell me the 'what is'—just the facts. Blood, strange behavior, limping?"

"There's blood and he's aware of us but on his side and not moving."

"Don't touch him and don't let your cats touch him. Lord knows if he ever had a rabies shot and I wouldn't want y'all hurt." And before I could tell him we'd already done that a hundred times over, he hung up.

I grabbed a towel, turned to Deidre who had followed me inside and watched me intently. "Stay put, honey. MJ's hurt and the doctor's coming. No need to have you out there too," I told her as I rushed out the door. She promptly followed me back outside onto the deck and sat, watching. I hurried to the high grass by the barn as my mind started reeling.

Oh, great—Cochon probably has rabies now. How long ago was his shot? What if MJ bites me? I'll get rabies! What if he dies? Maybe he's dead already! Oh, God, it'll break Cochon's heart.

But neither cat had moved. "MJ," I whispered as I got down on the damp grass and laid the big towel to the side. He made a small turn of his head toward me, eyes opening slightly, then closing again. His panting seemed loud, and I wondered if he had other injuries besides what I could see in the dim morning light. Cochon was as still as stone, watching the huge, black cat as he panted and moaned in a whisper, a sound that chilled me.

My heart hurt and I squeezed back tears. A sob hiccupped its way up and I swallowed it back down. Deidre appeared beside me and nuzzled my hip. The ultimate nurturer, she had an uncanny way of showing up when I was upset. I caressed her velvety head and looked out at the glorious beginning of dawn. I heard the small twitters of birds as they awakened. Overhead, a red-tailed hawk rode the thermals as a shaft of sunlight glinted off its chestnut-red tail feathers and broad, rounded wings. A slight breeze ruffled my hair, and the smell of earth and growing things entered my lungs. I took a deep breath and closed my eyes.

"Please let him live," I whispered.

Looking down at the still tableau that surrounded him, I realized at that moment that I loved this old stray. Not just because he had somehow transformed Cochon from a wimp into a confident representative of his own species, but also because he brought something special to all our lives. He seemed to stimulate life lessons for me over and over again. He was noble, good, and generous. I didn't want him to die.

Cochon's head shot up toward the driveway. I didn't hear a car motor but knew that didn't mean anything. The cats heard things long before I did. A few more seconds and I heard it. Then suddenly, while still on the street, the motor died and the car coasted almost silently into the driveway. I instinctively registered he'd done that to keep his noise level to a minimum so as not to scare MJ.

Doc Parsons got out quietly, leaving the car door open. An erect, slim figure with a spring in his step, he walked quickly toward our silent tableau. He knelt beside me, setting his black bag between us.

"Old fella, you've met your better on this one," he grunted as he deftly opened his bag and pulled out big gloves, a syringe, and a vial. "What's his name?"

"Michael Sabio Jordan Esquire the 1st ," I said. "We call him MJ for short," I added, watching him fill the syringe partway.

Doc grinned as he returned the vial to his bag. "That's quite a name—a physical wonder with wisdom to boot. Tells me a little of who I'm dealing with, doesn't it?" I nodded. "I'm going to give MJ a little shot to get him relaxed so we can move him. Could I borrow that towel you've brought for us?"

I handed it to him. "I didn't know it was for you. I just grabbed it as I ran out of the house. I don't know why... I wasn't thinking... I was just..." I shook my head and shut my mouth.

"You weren't thinking, but something was. Perfect choice," he chuckled. He put one glove on his left hand, then wrapped the towel around it. The glove went all the way to his elbow. Then slowly he stretched out his wrapped hand toward MJ's face. "Smell this, old son? It's a towel this nice lady brought just for you," and he moved it slowly, gently across MJ's cheek and down the side of his neck. MJ gurgled a scratchy sound, which might have been a meow. "I'm going to give you a bit 'a sleepin' juice now so you can rest," and his left hand stayed put but pressed more firmly. Suddenly, Doc slid a small syringe into MJ's hip with his right hand, depressing the plunger. His big, black head turned quickly to bite, but in his weakened condition, he gave up and gave the towel one pathetic lick. Doc set the syringe inside his open case, and MJ's head laid back down on the grass in exhaustion.

Doc removed the towel and glove, setting them aside. He added a top to the syringe, put it back in his case and shut it. "We'll sit a minute before we move him," he said, turning to face me. His eyes were clear, blue, and sparkling. He stuck out his right hand. "Doc Parsons. Privilege to meet you," he said, giving his head a tiny nod, like a bow. His grip was firm, his hand cool.

"And good to meet you, sir. I'm sorry to call you so early. I didn't know who else to call."

He shook his big head, thick with a mane of white hair. "No problem, young lady. There isn't anyone to call, least ways around here. I'm glad to help this big fella out. He's been around a long, long time in these parts. He killed a number of folk's chickens, mostly at Joss Hayward's till he got a decent chicken coop. MJ's got quite a reputation. Heard he fought a few dogs and a couple coyotes through the years too. And won. Quite the warrior."

"And pleased to meet him and the little lady too," he added, smiling toward Cochon, then Deidre. "Introductions?"

"This is Cochon," I said.

"Doesn't look like a pig to me!" he chuckled. "And this little lady?"

"Deidre." She meowed a small acknowledgement as I said her name and looked up at me.

"My, aren't you a beauty," he stated, and Deidre, ever a sucker for compliments, began to purr.

As Doc Parsons spoke directly to him, Cochon relaxed and sat down next to MJ again. "Cochon, I'm going to take your friend here with me for a bit and I promise to take good care of him, so don't you worry." MJ was sleeping soundly by now and Cochon stretched out, rubbing his head on MJ's ragged right ear.

Doc leaned back on his haunches, and I heard his joints crack. He laid the towel out, put both gloves on this time and carefully tucked an end of the towel under MJ's four legs. Then, he slowly scooped him up an inch off the ground and quickly yet gently laid him back down on the open towel. I saw blood in the grass, blood on MJ, blood on the towel. Folding it over him, Doc carefully picked up his bundle and started back to the car. I grabbed his black bag and trotted ahead of him to open the back car door. But Doc headed straight for the front seat, so I opened the passenger side, and he gently laid him down, took off the gloves and quietly shut the door as I set his bag on the back seat through the open window.

"I'll call you when I know more," he said, starting around the car. "I'll get him fully sedated with an IV and take some pictures. Hopefully all he got was a good mauling and his organs and bones are all right. Don't worry now, okay?" He stopped before he got into the car. He was waiting for me to answer.

"Sure, yeah. I'll try not to worry. Yes..." I answered, sounding somewhat addled as I peered in at MJ's bloody body through the dusty window. Doc didn't move, just stood there, looking at me over the top of the car. I looked up into his eyes, wondering what he was waiting for.

"I just want to be clear: don't *try* not to worry. *Don't* worry. If you do, it will scare Cochon. I can tell there's a special bond between those two, so he's going to be more sensitive than usual. If you're worrying, he'll get scared. Keep your mood up, okay? It'll help you, Cochon, and the little lady," he said, nodding toward Deidre. "You keep your mood up and it'll even help MJ here. Okay?"

I felt like I'd just been reassured yet lectured to in the kindest of ways. "Okay," I said, feeling mildly confused. Doc's house, which included his clinic, was only five miles away. But how could my worry reach across five long miles of farmland?

As he backed the car up, he waved, and I waved back. Aware of the precious cargo in his front seat, how could I *not* worry about that broken, bloody cat? What a ridiculous thing to say.

13

Good Medicine

"What a liberation to realize that the 'voice in my head'
is not who I am. Who am I then? The one who sees that."
– Eckhart Tolle

Returning to the house, I turned on the coffee pot, fed Deidre and Cochon, still bothered by Doc's words.

Keep my mood up? What in the world was he thinking? I'd like to know one little thing that's happy about any of this. What am I supposed to do? Smile some big, fake smile and dance around like nothing's wrong?

When I returned to the deck, worry about MJ immediately filled my mind.

How do you not worry? I'd worried my whole life. About everything—the cats, myself, people I loved, my health, other's health, finances, what people would do or think, even if a storm was coming. I'd worried about silly things and worthwhile things. Wasn't this a worthwhile worry?

People who didn't worry were either heartless or had that obscure thing called faith. They *believed* everything would be fine. But I'd had faith that loved ones would be fine.

And they hadn't been.

What good was faith then? It seemed no more than wishful thinking.

My worrying about the merits of worrying was interrupted by the crunching of footsteps on the gravel. And there was Emma, carrying a square pan covered with tin foil. As she approached, I stood up and set my coffee down, ready to help her. But she set the pan down on the little outside table and opened her arms. I moved into them, hugging her tightly, trying to get it out before I started crying.

"Did you see Doc was here? MJ's hurt really bad and he was bleeding and..." And then the crying began. She just held me, patting my back with those large, gnarled hands that could be so tender.

"Shhhh, shhh-shhh-shhhhhh," she whispered.

"He looked so *awful!*" I choked through the tears. "All covered with blood and not moving." My heart squeezed its pain out through my lips as I blubbered what I'd been afraid to say, "I'm afraid he'll die!" and the sobs came in full force. She squeezed me tighter, then backed up and reached into the pocket of her house-dress for a hanky. Her face was a soft landscape of tiny, concerned wrinkles. I blew my nose and sat down.

"I should have had Doc come over long before and at least check MJ over, given him a rabies shot. What if he dies? What will happen to Cochon? I should have never let him out in the first place. What was I *thinking* feeding a feral cat!" I sniffled. "I should have—"

Emma quietly interrupted my litany. "Thou shalt not should on thyself, honey," she said with mock seriousness.

It stopped me cold. I thought she'd said 'shit', not 'should', and it shocked me so much I stopped crying and just stared at her. Gus and Emma never cussed—in their world, swearing was for the lazy-minded.

A couple seconds ticked by before my mind caught up with my ears. I started laughing. "Oh, Emma," I exclaimed, wiping my eyes. "I thought you said thou shalt not s-h-i-t on thyself, not *should* on thyself!"

"'Bout the same thing, seems to me," she said, trying not to smile, but her brown eyes sparkled.

As she picked up the warm pan and rose, she studied my face and saw something. "No guilties now, honey. 'Should' (and she pronounced it very clearly) is a guilt maker. Once you think, 'I should have,' you feel guilty. And what's guilt? A feelin' whose sole purpose is to beat you up for what you should'a done. None of us knows what we *should'a* done. We only know what we did."

I heard the clattering sounds of silverware and dishes, and a minute later she returned with a mug of coffee and two forks in one hand, plus two small plates balanced in the other. Each was covered with a big, golden homemade cinnamon roll. The smells of yeast, cinnamon, and butter rose like sacred offerings into the morning air.

I pushed the hair out of my face, wiped my eyes again with the damp handkerchief, and took another ragged breath as I stared down at the most beautiful cinnamon roll I'd ever seen. It was perfection. *Who in the world gets up with the sun on a Tuesday morning and bakes these from scratch?* It was still warm and the pat of butter on top had melted, creating golden swirls on the blue plate.

We both chewed our first bite of heaven. "I'm so worried about him, Emma," I said.

"I know, honey. Let me tell you some things Doc shared with us about worry and such. He said it's a waste of perfectly good energy, one of the most useless emotions there is. It's just a pretty word for what folks calls anxiety or stress these days. I thought on that and asked myself if worry ever helped me in *any* way. Did all that frettin' ever help me decide anything, do anything, or figure anything out? No. Just left me with a knot in my belly.

"When we sit 'n stew our heads get confused, our *oomph* goes south, and we're useless—pure and simple. We get all stove up inside, you know? Paralyzed, stuck, and not worth a hoot. Only thing all that worryin' is good for is keepin' the Tums Antacid people in business," she chuckled.

I shook my head slowly. "But what kind of person am I if I don't worry about him? What does that say about *me*? It feels cold-hearted... like I don't care."

She chewed slowly, obviously relishing the early morning delicacy. "I beg to differ. Carin' and worryin' are opposites. When we're worried and stressed, we get all locked up inside. We sit and suffer, full 'o fear, wringin' our hands, all woe is me. On the other hand, carin' is love and that makes it a verb. And what's a verb?"

"An action word," I said, remembering this from Sunday dinner a few months ago. A couple minutes went by as we both sipped our hot coffee in the green of the morning, accompanied by the soft serenade of tiny rotund chickadees performing acrobatics in the bushes.

"It makes sense," I said. "It's just that... it seems to me I worry because I *do* care."

She nodded. "Most of us were raised to think that, like there's a prize for worryin'. If we win the prize, other folks will say how thoughtful we are or praise us for how much we worry, or we'll feel like we're doin' something. But the problem with 'I worry because I care' is it gives worry and love equal value. And that's just not true. The value of love outweighs worry a thousandfold. I can wring my hands about somethin' that may or may not happen up the road in the future—a future that doesn't even exist—or I can choose to *do* something and contribute to the situation right now, which *does* exist."

She walked inside to top off her coffee.

When she returned, I said, "You're right. When I'm worried, sometimes I literally get frozen by fear about what *might* happen. All I can think is, 'What if?' What if MJ is crippled? He wouldn't survive being kept inside. Not being outside would kill his spirit. What if he has rabies and now Cochon has them? What if he dies? What if Cochon gets sick or hurt because MJ's gone and not around to protect him? What if Cochon dies? Deidre would be left alone, and then what if..." I couldn't finish.

Emma chuckled. "Honey, that's a case of the 'what-ifs' if I ever heard one. Those two little words'll drive us crazy." She shrugged, laughing. "And think about it! The 'what if' we imagine is only a scary movie in our heads. Nothin' has happened. Nothin'! Yet here we go, gittin' all torn up about scary movies that don't exist. It might seem real in our minds, but the fact is it's all make-believe, fantasy... a *notion*, as my Ma used to call it."

"My 'what-ifs' are scary with terrible outcomes. They're never about something working out beautifully. They're full of fear about what happens if the movie comes true," I said.

She grinned and slowly shook her head. "Doc said if people would quit stewin' over the movies in their heads, he'd cut his patient load in half. I don't take for gospel *everything* Doc says, but I figured he's seen a lot in his time and thought he was probably right on this one."

Cochon woke up and came by to rub against our legs. Emma smiled and shook her head in wonder as she gently reached down to pet him. "My, my, look at that. Once upon a time, I didn't think I'd get to see him, let alone pet him. Isn't he strong and beautiful!"

As I watched her stroking Cochon, I was overcome for the hundredth time by the sheer impossibility of his physical changes that clashed against what my mind said I *should* be seeing. It was incomprehensible. And magical. As I watched the two of them and these thoughts went through my mind, I realized I wasn't worrying about MJ.

"Emma, just now as I watched you and thought of Cochon and the miraculous changes he's gone through, I forgot all about MJ for a minute. The 'shoulds', the scary movies, and the 'what ifs' disappeared."

She nodded and held up a finger. "I do three things to stop that anxiety nonsense. First, I remember I got eyeballs. The Good Lord made these eyes to look outward, not inward. I change my focus from me and my so-called problems to what's goin' on around me right now, like you just did. Feels good, doesn't it?"

"It does. And it's simple," I said.

"It's just a matter of changin' ingrown attention to outward attention. I swear, ingrown attention, watchin' all those movies, hurts worse than an ingrown toenail." She grimaced.

"I just hope I don't get all caught up in it and forget."

"But you *will* forget. And you'll also remember. We just keep practicin'. You don't learn to tie your shoe or fly an airplane by doing it once. Doc says that practicin' is like galoshes; the more we practice, the more protection we got when we wander around in the muck up here." She tapped her forehead. "I do whatever helps me to come back to right here, right now. I stop tryin' to go up that road to where I don't belong by makin' my mind focus on what's a'goin' on right now."

"That's where stopping the 'shoulds' and 'what ifs' matters. Keeps you here, right?" I asked.

"Yes, ma'am. The second thing I do"—she held up two fingers—"is get up and get movin'." She stood and picked up our empty plates. "Sometimes just breakin' that paralysis is as simple as doin' the dishes or makin' the bed. It's good for the soul and breaks that feelin' of bein' all froze up and unable to make a decision."

She looked out at the bur oak leaning toward the little stream of irrigation water that ran through the canal, then turned to me, holding up her third finger. "Third thing I do is remind myself I'm just fine right now. It might sound crazy, but no matter what's happenin', I'm right fine, I'm okay, *right now.* Pure and simple." She nodded her head.

"How did you learn these things?" I asked, hoping it was quick and easy.

She grinned. "Life gave me lessons *and* also provided answers if I wanted to work the lessons a bit. It was after Ronnie died and I had a lotta time to think on things. Gus and I finally talked with Doc, who is the wisest man I know. He didn't tell us what to do or think, just offered ways to see life a little different and said to check 'em out for ourselves. I was tired of bein' a worrywart, of bein' afraid and feelin' sad. So, I practiced a few simple things. It was hard 'cause our heads are so noisy. But the more I practiced, the easier it got. At first it was like tryin' to herd a bunch of wild birds flyin' around up here." She patted her head. "But remember, honey, just 'cause one lands, it doesn't mean we have to let it stay and build a nest." She chuckled.

As if on cue, the screech of a bird sounded high above. We watched as a red-tail hawk circled in ever-widening arcs, hunting breakfast. "Maizie down at Isleta Pueblo told me the hawk brings good medicine. It increases our ability to focus, just what we been talkin' about."

I was glad of the hawk. I figured I could use a little focusing medicine if I was going to learn to stop worrying so much.

She continued, "I heard Doc saved a red-tail hawk's life last winter. Doubt there's a critter he hasn't helped, so that ol' cat's in mighty good hands. If anybody can save 'im, that man can. He's a miracle worker for certain. MJ wouldn't be the first animal—or human for that matter—to return nice as you please from death's door." Emma drank the last sip of her coffee.

"Before you go, Doc told me if I worried it would affect Cochon and MJ. Cochon makes sense. The cats feel it when I'm sad or troubled. But MJ? I don't understand—he's at Doc's, over five miles away. Do you know what he meant?"

"Well, Doc says some strange things. Who's to know? Maybe our thoughts and feelins travel out a ways... like when you're thinkin' of someone, and they call you out of the blue. Or somebody comes to mind, and you get a letter from 'em, or you think of a friend and there they are in the grocery store. Haven't you had that happen?" I nodded, thinking it had happened countless times over the years.

"I don't understand much of this world, but let's pretend a minute. If MJ *could* feel what you feel all the way over to Doc's, what would you *want* him to feel?" she asked, setting her empty cup down.

I didn't hesitate. "Love. And gratitude for all he's done to bring Cochon out of his shell. I surely wouldn't want him to feel all the worry *I'm* feeling. But how do I make sure I send only the right thoughts?"

Emma reached out and squeezed my hand. "Maybe thinkin' isn't as important as feelin'. Seems thinkin's job is to help you decide which feelin' you want. Pick one: Interested? Delighted? Peaceful? Grateful? Loving? Without the worry you can feel whatever you choose. Don't get lost in thinkin' your message. *Feel* it. Seems folks don't hear much of what we say, but they sure know how they feel when they're with us."

We were quiet, listening to the sound of children's laughter at the other end of the street, the barking of Barry Mackland's dog, Ferrari, in a nearby field, and the rustling of leaves from the whispering breeze. Emma smiled, a peaceful look on her face. "When I consider my feelins radiatin' outward a ways, it feels like I'm sending a package. I wanna make sure they're happy when they open it.

"Take my sister. I can't be with her in Arkansas, but I can stop a moment and feel my love for her, my gratitude, and how proud I am of her. I don't know how far thoughts and feelins go, but I wanna make sure no matter how far they reach, whatever I'm sending is somethin' worthy to be give away."

"I like that," I said, imagining a wrapped package with a large, satin bow traveling through the ethers.

She bent down, kissed my cheek, and said, "And remember, none of us knows how far our thoughts and feelins can travel. This ol' world is a pretty strange and magical place, seems to me. Let yourself radiate like the sun. You have lots of goodness to give out, more than you know. Let it shine, missie." As she walked across the driveway toward their home, I could hear her softly singing an old gospel song, "This Little Light of Mine."

After she'd gone, I closed my eyes and thought of MJ. Because my educated mind knew it was smart and powerful, I created the most intense curative images I could and tried to send them. I conjured laser beams, golden arrows, and Peregrine Falcons diving full throttle to drop shimmering healing messages at MJ's feet.

It didn't work. Probably because I didn't believe it. Instead of feeling more at ease, I felt like I was moving into a dark, grey ocean in a howling storm. My eyes watered as I felt myself sliding backwards.

So, I gave up being smart and simply did what Emma said—got moving, washed the dishes from those exquisite rolls and now-cold coffee. When a "what-if" thought crept in, I reminded myself it was about a future that didn't even exist. As awful pictures arose in my mind of Doc calling with bad news, or Cochon grieving, or me grieving, I said aloud, "That's make-believe; fantasy." The more I focused, the calmer I felt.

I even started grinning at myself a little. What an active imagination I had! Slowly, the seas began to calm and new feelings of being at ease broke to the surface. The noise in my head diminished to dull whispers. Internal movies disappeared like wisps of clouds. A sense of peace stilled the waters.

I picked up the garden bucket from the sunroom and returned outside into the fresh New Mexico morning. Breathing deeply, I knelt before the marigolds in the front that bordered the deck. As I pressed my fingers into the damp, dark earth, pulling gently on the unwanted weeds, I felt stronger. Lighter. Quieter. The cats awoke and came to watch, batting bugs and sniffing the little pile of discarded greenery. Time passed unnoticed as I pruned and replanted and fertilized.

At some point, the kaleidoscope made a tiny turn and…

Click.

At that moment, I wasn't the thoughts in my mind. I was the watcher of those thoughts. I was strangely present, aware of not only humming a song, but also how it felt in my throat and body to hum. I was there but unidentified with even my own body. I was aware of peering out of my own eyes, moving my muscles, even aware of the taste of morning air.

Something alien stirred as I found a place inside I thought I had lost. Later, when I tried to give it a name, the only word that felt right was "home."

14

Waiting Is

"Forever – is composed of Nows –"
– Emily Dickenson

I relaxed into the morning, accepting MJ was in the best hands anyone could ask for. As I was scanning the morning newspaper, I noticed an ad for a funeral home. And in the blink of an eye a thought arose that MJ might be dead. A vignette followed of Doc at the door, holding MJ's body wrapped in a blanket and ready for burial. The movies had begun.

Thanks to Emma, I only spent a few seconds feeling afraid. Instead, I turned my focus away from the pictures and took a deep breath, whispering, "I am here... that's illusion, not fact. I don't know the future—period," and the movie faded. I realized watching my thoughts, rather than getting caught up in them, made a difference.

Yet, it surprised me how quickly these ideas appeared. I mistakenly thought feeling peaceful and present would prevent any anxiety. How natural it was for me to think the worst; it was an awareness that surprised and saddened me.

Also surprising was to see how automatically I bought suggestions. Without our talk this morning, I would be lost in that same old place of champion worrier right now, all because of a simple newspaper ad. How many of my thoughts were knee-jerk reactions, brought on by mere association to something I'd watched or read, a song I'd heard, or words spoken? My suggestibility surprised me.

I looked at Cochon lying in the grass with Deidre and thought how it wasn't just him who was changing. Observing myself, I knew I was changing too.

I stood up and stretched and the cats and I went indoors as the morning began to warm. It was my first Bosque summer living in an adobe home. I did what others recommended: shut the windows I'd left open overnight, then pulled the blinds over the sunniest ones. That routine, plus the tile floors and spinning overhead fans, kept the house comfortable in the heat of summer. At night I reversed the process. I learned to work with the environment I lived in. We were comfortable in this agreeable land.

For the umpteenth time, I looked at my watch. It had been almost four hours since Doc had left with a bloody MJ. I wasn't good at waiting. It was boring, a waste of time. Whenever I had to wait, I'd thumb through a magazine, or read a book, or bring work with me. I wanted to be busy and productive. I also wanted to be seen that way. How odd would it be for someone to be in a waiting room and do nothing but sit and stare? As I waited for his call, I remembered an experience I'd had at university over twenty years ago.

It was the late sixties and I was part of the hippie generation. Much of the student body participated in the already strong movement of hundreds of thousands of young people across the US and even in Europe who were calling for change. We discussed, explored, and debated. We signed petitions. We marched against the Vietnam War and marched for equality for women, the second-class citizens of the world. We called for civil rights and an end to poverty. We worked against consumerism, blind acceptance of the authority du jour, and the status quo. We wanted peace, love, and rock and roll. We were young, energetic, naive, and full of hope.

In school I studied psychology and philosophy. I explored the world's religions, all seemingly fingers on the hand of God. I yearned to understand. What was my life for? What was its meaning? What was my purpose in being here? What could I do to make a difference? I was an endless question mark.

One morning, as I walked home on my way from an early class, I wandered into a quiet neighborhood, drawn by distant music. I arrived at a two-story bungalow where sonorous chanting filled the air. I stood outside, mesmerized as notes danced in acapella harmonies that sounded like angel voices, sung in words I didn't understand. When it stopped, a young man came outside and invited me in. He said they were having a class and their Rōshi had come from Japan—a great honor for them—and I was invited to attend. Just like that, a stranger off the street was welcomed into their home.

I removed my sandals and joined him to sit in the back of a classroom scattered with flat pillows on the floor instead of desks. Everyone was silent, anticipating a spiritual lesson from their teacher that was scheduled to begin in five minutes. We were all ready.

But no Rōshi appeared. After about thirty minutes, a few people began to fidget, then a few more. At the hour mark, someone whispered, "Should we check on the master? Maybe he was taken ill? He's old and had a long trip. Maybe he forgot?" But no one did.

I began to doze, leaning against the back wall. The clock ticked in the silent room. Several sat in meditation poses. One snored faintly. Over an hour later, footsteps were heard in the corridor. We all came to attention and a small man quietly walked into the room. Everyone, including me, sat up straight, glad the waiting was finally over. He pressed his hands together in a prayer-like fashion and looked at each of us, one by one. He had the most beatific smile I had ever seen. His eyes held a delicate balance of enthusiasm and compassion. He bowed deep and slow and stood back up, perhaps his way of honoring our presence.

The silence was profound. No one moved a muscle. I think we all held our breath as we awaited his wisdom. Then he looked out at us and clearly said in his soft yet substantive voice, "Waiting is."

He smiled his enigmatic smile, bowed, and walked out the door, a sublime little Japanese man in a black robe and white anklet socks.

That's all he said.

It was so quiet I could hear the breeze whisper to the treetops through the open windows. I thought it murmured, *"What happened?"* Slowly, the room unwound itself as the participants looked around at each other and stood up. I couldn't tell if they were awed or disappointed or irritated. Perhaps a little of each.

I slipped out, miffed I'd wasted two hours. For that? He hadn't said anything. But over the years, whenever I waited—for a friend, or at the dentist's office, or for a letter to arrive, or the phone to ring—his words came back like a tiny pebble in my shoe. But I never understood.

Until now.

Click.

And all at once I did.

I saw two kinds of waiting. The usual one brought an expectation of completion. That kind of waiting focused on the future. It was restless and dissatisfied, because until "this" was done, there was no way to move on to "that." Waiting *wanted* something as it tapped its toes impatiently. It was unaware of the present because it was focused on what it wanted, needed, expected, wished or hoped for. Or demanded. While waiting, the waiter was antsy, filled with boredom or frustration, anxiety or anger, because that for which they were waiting hadn't happened yet. It served no purpose, a pointless expenditure of energy.

However, there was another kind of Waiting. In its purest form, I saw it as "Waiting" with a capital W. This kind of Waiting opened a door to a place where the Waiter could notice, observe, and be present. This Waiting with a capital W was its own thing complete unto itself. Like sitting still doing nothing, humming, or staring out the window. It could exist alone, without need for a future.

"Whatcha doing?"

"Humming."

"Okay."

And no one asks, "Why are you humming? What are you humming for? Are you humming for someone? What are you doing when you finish humming? How long will you be doing it? What happens when you stop?" Because humming is complete unto itself. It is its own experience, needing nothing.

So is Waiting. All by itself it exists. It is without direction, pushing, or focusing. It is the state of being present without desire. Seeing Waiting this way had a kind of innocence, a beauty and grace. I wondered if this ability to be content in the moment was also a part of the state of being called Ho'zho' that Jake had talked about. I wondered if this was another way to walk in beauty.

At that moment I stopped waiting for Doc to call. Being here was enough. All was well just like it was. I let go.

And as has happened so many times in my life following a change of perception, the lesson book closed. The phone rang.

"Hello?"

"Hi, glad you're there. Doc here. We got MJ anesthetized and clipped the fur around that wound so I could take a look-see." He paused.

"Is it bad?"

"Not bad, but he had a few puncture wounds from talons, one that tore a bit. My guess is he got in a tussle with a Great Horned Owl." He started chuckling. "As limber and wily as MJ is, it may not have gotten the hold on him it needed. I doubt that owl knew how big and heavy he was when it tried to get dinner."

I listened for the punchline. *Dead? Paralyzed? Dying?*

"And?" I asked.

"And every puncture was cleaned. The ragged parts of where his skin tore were vital, so I trimmed off the rough edges and closed it up. No broken bones, no organ damage. He has two sets of sutures on the tear: a deeper set and an upper set. I use absorbable ones because I want to avoid him being knocked out again to remove the stitches. Not even the best minds know what happens to people, let alone animals, when they're anesthetized."

"So, he's going to live. He'll be okay and come back soon?"

"I don't know the future, so let's take it one step at a time. Right now, I just want to see how he does when he wakes up. It will depend on the healing of the puncture wounds and the little tear. I've got some shots to give him—antibiotic, rabies, RCP. Let's put it this way. We'll do our best and the rest will be up to MJ and whatever magic runs this big old school called Life." I could hear him smiling. "I'll call you when I know more. Anything else?"

I paused, not sure if I should say anything, then did. "Doc, speaking of school, Emma shared some ideas this morning about not worrying, a lesson I could stand to learn. But I've got to admit, it's kind of hit and miss right now."

"That's all right. Hit and miss is perfect. It means you're paying attention. Otherwise, you wouldn't know you missed. You've had a lifetime of worrying about what might happen. If you're like the rest of the world, you've created some real horror movies in your mind. Did you see *Jaws?*"

"I did. Pretty scary. I was in a knot through most of it."

"It was certainly one of the most nerve-wracking movies I've ever seen. There's only one Steven Spielberg. The man's a master at his craft. Don't try to take his job, okay? Leave the scary movies to the professionals."

It was my turn to smile. "Maybe my movies aren't quite *Jaws*, but they get pretty scary."

"There's an adage," he said, "old but true: practice makes perfect. Don't know about the perfection part, but staying out of the muck gets easier the more we remember to wear our galoshes. And practicing is the galoshes." I was hearing this for the second time today and I knew I could use the reminder. He continued. "Rest assured if there's anything significant, I'll call you immediately. How's Cochon?"

"Seems fine, just sleeping a lot."

"That's when most of the healing happens. Isn't Life smart? Make it a great day now."

"I will. You too." And he was gone.

I went to my small office and began writing checks, paying bills, and addressing envelopes for birthday cards. Deidre came in and wound about my ankles until I stopped to stroke her back and rub her ears and face. "Where's Cochon?" I asked, remembering they had both been asleep on the couch. She ignored my question as she luxuriated in her cat massage. "Still passed out, huh?" I said to her and returned to satisfying the creditors as she wandered away.

Almost an hour later, I finished and headed to the kitchen to make a late lunch. As I passed the couch, I noticed Deidre had gone back to sleep, curled in a ball with her fluffy tail covering her eyes. But Cochon's soft, grey body wasn't there. I reached into the fridge for the tuna salad, and he suddenly meowed in a loud voice.

I started, almost dropping the container. His meowing, talking, and purring still took me by surprise. I turned toward the sound where he perched on the windowsill, staring outside. I walked over and he lightly jumped down to stand by the door. He looked at me and meowed again. "Of course." I opened the door. "Just a minute and I'll join you," I called, walking back to the kitchen to put the tuna away. I just wasn't hungry.

When I stepped outside, he was already gone. I looked toward the little canal, then the high grass by the barn. A small fearful feeling nudged my belly. "Not going there," I said firmly to myself and dismissed the scary movie. Before settling into my favorite chair, I looked out to see if the flag was down and the mailman had come.

And there was Cochon, sitting tall, staring down the street, as still as the mailbox post beside him.

The cats usually stayed away from the end of our drive. Though I never saw a car unless someone visited Gus, Emma, or me, I didn't worry about them getting hit because their attention was attuned to the wild things—the small, natural wonders that inhabited our quiet slice of heaven. I watched him for a minute, then heard a girl's sweet, lilting voice call, "Hey, kitty. Kitty-kitty-kitty? Whatcha doin', waitin' for the mail?"

I watched as Carlita Hernandez, the girl Emma called Carlie, walked into view. Carlita was the oldest of the Sanchez children. She married Miguel Hernandez, who went into the service when they found out she was pregnant. We hadn't met and had only waved at each other since she moved back home to live in the bosom of her kin.

Today, she was wearing a baggy man's shirt, sleeves rolled up, and tan shorts. Her long black hair glistened in the sun as she bent over and proffered a finger to Cochon. He met her eyes and waited. A few seconds passed and he craned his neck out to sniff her finger. Then, he stood up and commenced giving her whole hand a good whiff. She evidently passed muster because he rubbed his cheek against her hand and then her bare leg. "Oh, you're so pretty," she said and reached down to pet him. She saw me from the corner of her eye. "Is this your cat? I can't tell if it's a girl or boy," she laughed.

I walked across the yard to the mailbox, and we made our introductions. "Not sure anybody ever owns a cat, but, yes, he's ours. His name is Cochon, and he used to be shy." Then Cochon, the wonder cat, laid down on his side to expose his tummy. "But not anymore, it seems," I added. She glided her small hand softly and slowly up and down his front several times as he stretched his full length, forming a parenthesis. Once again, I was awed by whatever happened to make him so amenable to strangers.

Just then Emma opened her front door. "Hi, ladies!" she called and walked over to join us. "Thanks for dropping by, Carlie. I've got your blouse almost done and just wanna check the shoulders. I see you've met Cochon—isn't he grand?" She smiled like a proud grandmother, then looked at me. "You think he's waitin' for MJ to come back? The cats don't come out by the road."

"I don't know, Emma." Though his behavior was puzzling, I thought she might be right.

Carlie had bent down to continue petting and stroking Cochon. She looked up at me. "He's so beautiful. He reminds me of a Female Rain." She could tell I didn't understand. "My girlfriend is Diné—Navajo. She said there are Male Rains and Female Rains. The Male Rains are huge downpours that give a ton of water but don't last long, lots of dark grey-black clouds, thunder and lightning. The Female Rains are lighter rains that last longer. They're softer and gentler with lighter grey clouds. Cochon is light grey and gentle, like a Female Rain. Aren't you, kitty?" He stared at her, listening to the new attributions she had given him.

Emma turned to me. "Any word from Doc yet?" Just then, Gus came out of the garage beside their house and walked toward us, wiping his hands.

"MJ has been stitched up and he's sleeping. Doc will call me when he gets a better sense after the anesthesia wears off. He thinks a Great Horned Owl grabbed him, unaware of how strong and flexible he was. He said there were talon punctures."

"I told Emma that," Gus said in his gruff voice as he walked toward us, wiping his hands on an old towel. "That ol' cat is not jes powerful strong, he's an acrobat. Saw 'im jump off'a the cotton-wood from 'bout six feet or so 'n twist round, every bit of 'im ripplin' muscle." He kept wiping his hands, still smeared with grease from the tractor. "The Great Horned is huge—eyes like telescopes and talons with a grip stronger than any human alive. That ugly ol' cat is plain lucky he didn't get grabbed jes right.

Would'a crushed his spine like a matchstick," he said, wincing a little.

Carlie folded her arms across her chest and made a face. Gus looked down at her slightly protruding belly that was obvious now that she'd flattened the big shirt against herself. "*There's* that youngin'! Won't be long, now, missie," he said and grinned ear-to-ear. "Got a mess over there. See y'all later." He sauntered back to the waiting tractor.

She patted her tummy. "Tomorrow is five months. Only four to go." She was so tiny, short and delicate boned, that she looked like she had six months to go, not four. "Emma's blouse will be so much prettier than my dad's work shirts," she giggled, then asked, "Who is MJ? I'm sorry he's hurt." A look of sadness touched her face.

I told her about MJ, our Thanksgiving gift, who had gone from being fully feral to trusting my food and Cochon's friendship. "*That little guy*"—I nodded toward Cochon—"was about half that size a few months ago, scared of everything, and couldn't talk until MJ came into our world. It's a..." and I stopped, slowly shaking my head. I had no word. But Carlie did.

"Es un milagro... a miracle," she said, wide-eyed, in a hushed voice. She squatted down by Cochon and spoke quietly in Spanish. "Tienes un curandero. Él te ha bendecido," she said, caressing his head. I asked her what she said. "I told him he has a healer who has blessed him. He's very loved to receive such a gift." Cochon gave a small meow as if in agreement, walked behind the mailbox post and laid down in the shade. I think each of us felt there was something holy about the moment, as Carlie verbalized what we knew but hadn't said.

Emma hugged her. "Thank you, honey. Okay now, let's go finish your blouse." They headed back, Emma's arm around Carlie's narrow shoulders and Carlie's arm around Emma's large waist.

"Come on, Cochon," I told him as I started walking back to the house. But he didn't follow. I hesitated, then walked back and sat down beside him on the grass. I smoothed his side and scrubbed his ear and face. He turned to lick my hand. "My sweetest boy," I whispered, stroking, smoothing, aware of a woodpecker tapping on a tree, a car door slamming far away, the sound of laughter from the Sanchez kids down the street. A jet flew overhead silently, its contrail marking the passage of time and space.

We looked in each other's eyes. "You teach me to be a better friend," I said. "You teach me that Waiting is, that love is about action, not words... that presence in this moment, on this day, at this time... is enough."

He licked his paw, rubbed it over his cheek and nose, then relaxed again. I smiled and massaged the top of his head and ears, "Because of you and MJ, it seems every day I'm reminded that life is filled with unknowable wonder. Just look at you! You're growing, you're talking, you're becoming. I am beyond joy to see you step fully into your life." I stood up and he raised his head, watching me. "I can't begin to tell you how the magic, the sweetness, the purity of all this touches my heart." Tears filled my eyes.

My mamaw said we were to never wipe away tears of joy, only tears of sorrow. I left them untouched to make their own contrails down my cheeks as I returned to the house where Deidre waited in the doorway.

Cochon stayed until almost sundown, Waiting with a capital W.

Waiting without expectation, without need, without want.

15

Water Brothers

"Each friend represents a world in us,
a world possibly not born until they arrive,
and it is only by this meeting that a new world is born."
– Anaïs Nin

The next day, I refused to worry, ignoring the mental noise and horror flicks in my head. I didn't wait, I just kept focusing on what was in front of me. Doc Parsons didn't call until around 2pm.

He got right to the point. "Doc here. I've got an update on MJ."

"Good, I've been looking forward to your call. How's he doing?"

"All is well. No redness or swelling around the sutures, no abscesses or infection so far, and no fever. He doesn't know what to make of a litter box, so he peed a little in the corner on some cut newspaper and scratched around. Good to see. However, he's lapped only a tiny bit of water, and won't eat. Though each patient is different, usually at least a little of their appetite returns twenty-four hours after surgery." He paused, then chuckled. "I'm a fair cook and he got my special homemade cat food: healthy, balanced, made with ground chicken from Carol and Dave's. Great chickens too. They let their bunch roam around, peck in the dirt, eat bugs, forage... MJ wouldn't even sniff it."

"Sorry he turned down your gourmet food," I said, smiling while remembering I was almost out of eggs. "Maybe he'll eat tomorrow. Are you worried?" As soon as I asked, I knew it was a dumb question.

"No," he chuckled. "If I worry, I might miss something. I'm just watching. I learned a long time ago that life has its own schedule for healing. If I try to rush and push and change it, it feels like inter-ference. I just get in the way and the healing takes longer. On the other hand, if I pay attention and keep my eyes open, whatever is needed will show itself. It's a good time to be patient." I was quiet, trying to figure out how all this watching would work if MJ was slowly dying of something he couldn't see.

As if reading my mind, he said, "Seems a little laissez-faire, doesn't it? But if you can trust me, if the time comes for me to insert myself, know I won't hesitate. Otherwise, I want to be respectful of how he and life are working to restore balance."

Feeling relieved, I said, "*Please* tell me I can do something."

"You can. Hold on a minute and let me get a pencil." I heard a drawer rattle open and close, followed by a soft grunt as he reached for something. "Okay, got it. Tell me what you usually feed him. Be specific and I'll write."

I felt strangely honored to be asked to help this man. Plus, it felt good to *do* something. "I know they're carnivores, so I give him cooked beef, chicken, or turkey, either oven-roasted or cooked in the Crock Pot. Fish if I have it. I mash in a little carrot or squash. Most of the time he ignores the vegetables. I grow my own alfalfa sprouts, so if I have some, I chop 'em up and toss them in. He likes those. I don't season the meat or vegetables. I haven't for years, ever since my first cat. That help?"

"It does. And did you grind the meat or chop it?"

"You know, he basically wolfed it down whatever way I gave it to him. Sometimes the meat was already chopped or shredded. Sometimes I tore off chunks." I started laughing. "That guy swallows his food whole, no matter what size it is."

"Did you give him skin or juice from the meat?" he asked.

"I never season meat, so both. Also, he didn't seem to care if it was warm or cold." I paused. "I think that's it, Doc. Not a very interesting diet, but it's put some meat on his bones, and he looks a lot better than last November."

"Ever feed him raw meat?" he asked.

"A few pieces of raw roast beef once, but he didn't seem to prefer it. Which was odd because I figured being feral, he only ate raw food."

"Well, we just don't know. He may have eaten dog food left out or scraps given to chickens or gotten into garbage bins. The old boy was resourceful—that we *do* know." Again he chuckled. "I'll call you when he either eats or it's time to intervene. Talk soon." He hung up.

That evening, Cochon was restless. Several times, he went to the door, came back to us, wandered the house. When he wanted out, Deidre and I joined him. He went straight to the mailbox and sat, once again staring down the street.

I squinted to see him in the dusk. Soon he laid down. Though Deidre avoided the street area, this evening she joined him and stayed beside him until the sky had relinquished its last wisp of burnished gold. They wandered back in the dark and we went in for the night. He seemed to have used up his restless energy and just wanted to sleep. I didn't know if he was tired or disappointed, or perhaps even sad. I couldn't tell.

The next morning, he started pacing again as he looked out the window, wandering back and forth in circles from the back office to the greenhouse to the front door and back again. As I was washing breakfast dishes, suddenly he yowled so loud I dropped a cup. I wiped my sudsy hands on my jeans and rushed over. "Hey, what's wrong, buddy?" His loud, drawn-out meow sounded like he was in pain. I carefully picked him up, feeling his body for bumps, tender spots, or wetness. My frantic mind looked for sources—broken glass, a spider bite, a snake in the house, internal organ failure. He briefly let me hold and check his body, then struggled to get down. Then he yowled again. And the phone rang.

"Good morning, Doc here and—"

I cut him off. "I was just going to call you. Cochon has yelled twice, like he's in pain. He's never done that before. It was like a scream. Can I bring him in?" As I was talking, I'd walked into my office and gotten the cat carrier to set by the door.

"Actually, I was calling to see if you would bring him anyway. Also, I told you I'd let you know if it's time to insert myself. It's time. So, please bring the bowl you usually feed MJ in, filled with his regular breakfast."

"You bet. I'll see you in a few minutes." I hung up.

What if Cochon had a twisted intestine? A blockage? Was he having a heart attack? Going to have a seizure? I was chiding myself for not knowing more about cat anatomy as a scary scene flitted by of him dying before we reached the clinic.

I grabbed MJ's old porcelain bowl and put a small amount of chicken meat, skin, and broth in it from last night's dinner. I covered it in foil, grabbed my keys, and called for Cochon. No answer. "Cochon?" I called in my calmest voice, trying not to sound desperate. Still no answer. I bent down to put the bowl in the back of the carrier and... there he was, already in it, looking up at me. "Well, look at you," I whispered, staring in at his waiting form.

Neither cat liked the carrier. They were trapped in a moving box going to the unknown. But this morning, Cochon was not only ready, he was impatient. I closed the carrier door and suddenly time slowed down as I looked at him.

His recent behavior—the restlessness, the meandering from room to room, the waiting by the mailbox and staring out the windows—all coalesced into the knowing that his yowls weren't from pain of the body. They were the sounds of longing; the pain of the heart.

His vocalizing was urgent. The crescendo of his restlessness had arrived. And somehow, I understood without words, without logic or proof. I knew in every fiber of my being that Cochon was getting a message from his friend: *"Come! Help me!"* It was time for action.

This knowing, this awareness, came to me in the time it took to live in the space between two heartbeats. So much magic had happened since MJ had come into our lives that I didn't second guess it. I realized I was witnessing a demonstration of a connection so strong that when one needed help, the other felt it. Even five miles away.

I set the carrier and MJ's food on the front seat. As I drove, Cochon was quiet. He was content, a departure from his normal "The sky is falling!" carrier behavior... content even without Deidre, who was ever present by his side to reassure him. It seemed like a long time ago he had been so small and so afraid of life.

We pulled in and Doc came out to meet us. As I was undoing my seatbelt, he bent down by my window. "He's not hurt, Doc." I hesitated, then went ahead anyway. "As crazy as this sounds, I think MJ needs him and he feels it. Sorry for the panic."

"Don't ever apologize. Are you sure you don't want me to take a look?"

I nodded. "I'm sure. There's something going on here that is way beyond me."

He looked at Cochon, then at me, nodding. "Okay, then let's begin by you two staying put while I see if he'll eat first." I handed him the bowl. "I'll be back shortly," he said and walked swiftly back to the house.

It was quiet, surrounded by fields and pasture on all sides. The large, arched front gate made of willow was left open and I could see inside. Flagstones created a flat, smooth, and wide walkway to his front door. Surrounding the flagstones was a large courtyard, filled with an artful blend of native plants, flowers, cedar and fruit trees.

His home was a long, sprawling, orange-brown adobe, the color of rich clay. The front door faced east with windows along that side of the house. Hanging flower baskets hung from the arched entrance to the home. It was peaceful. I took a deep breath and leaned back, closing my eyes, listening to tiny finches converse about the simplicity of life as small breezes danced through the leaves.

I felt deeply relaxed. A long-forgotten memory surfaced of feeling this way at my grandparent's farm in West Virginia. My siblings, cousins, and I would leave the Middle Farm, as it was called, and walk down the winding dirt path to the creek, pro-nounced 'crick' by my papaw. It seemed wide to us, deep enough for swimming in a few places and shallow enough for playing in the rest. Dotted along the edges were huge, granite boulders that rose like giant behemoths out of Sugar Creek. They were so big that some stretched halfway to the other side and you could have easily fit all ten of us on one boulder. They were ancient, worn smooth by time, wind, and water. After wearing ourselves out in the cold mountain stream, we would each choose a warm boulder to lie on, resting as we dried out in the summer sun.

In those days my world was still magical. I sensed the boulder I laid on was alive. Lying flat, I could feel it breathe, so slowly I had to be utterly still to feel each long inhalation. When it exhaled, it released a feeling of exquisite peace from its stone lungs into the palms of my hands, that would course through my arms, up into my face and ears and hair, and spread like warm honey to my toes. Skin against rock, my palms were the doorway that accepted the giant stone's breath of peace and the messages it whispered…*"beautiful… safe… good…"* It filled me up with a happiness and serenity gleaned from no other experience.

I never did share my secret. Until now. Partly because I didn't want people to think I was crazy. But also because I instinctively knew that when magic happened to me, talking about it assured it would never happen again. I kept it to myself in those days of wonderment.

I felt like that now, that same sense of serenity while something magical was happening. I was suspended in an enchanted moment in time. There was a rightness to Cochon's demanding behavior, MJ's pulling need, Doc's availability, all of it... a certain harmony and order that nothing in the world could alter. It felt as if something had been set into motion the day MJ arrived last Thanksgiving. My job was to pay attention, watch, and be open to what was happening. Because this wasn't only about Cochon and MJ—it was about me, Deidre, Doc, Jake, Emma and Gus, Carlita, even those I hadn't met yet. I didn't know what was happening, but it had a sense of the sacred about it.

I heard crunching footsteps on the gravel and sat up as Doc approached. "Ready?" I asked.

"I'll take the carrier if you like," he said, and I let him.

We entered the house by a side door under a sign that simply said "Doc's". The small waiting room had a wooden desk, overshadowed by a large cork board with so many pictures of people and their pets that they were in layers. There were two chairs, a water crock, paper cups, and a short bookshelf stuffed with everything from comic books to classics. A tiny coffee table held a stack of New Mexico Magazine copies. The top one was August and had a photograph of a Nambe pueblo boy with parts of the American flag painted on his face, titled 'First Americans.' It was beautiful but made me sad to know how many had forgotten that truth. Next to the magazines was MJ's food I'd brought, obviously untouched.

He picked it up and handed it to me. "He wouldn't eat, and it's been over forty-eight hours. He's barely drinking. His wounds aren't making the progress I'd like, and he's lethargic, sleeps most of the time, and ignores normal stimuli. Let's see if Cochon can help."

He opened another door to a small, sunny room with two skylights and several animal cages, chairs, and two big toyboxes, one marked "I LOVE MY DOG" and the other "I LOVE MY CAT." On both, the "O" in "LOVE" had been replaced with a big red heart. The largest cage was so big it could have held an English Mastiff. Doc pointed to it. As I approached, bowl in hand like a supplicant with an offering, MJ raised his head to look at me. "Hey, buddy, I've sure missed you," I told him in my cooing, quiet voice.

Just then, Cochon let out his huge yowl and we all jumped. I think MJ was startled the most. He suddenly stood up on wobbly legs and gave a series of ragged meows back. I could feel Doc's excitement as he quickly brought Cochon, who continued to yowl, and sat the carrier down with its door open. We moved away and watched as a tiny miracle took place.

They both quit talking and looked at each other. Then Cochon sniffed the outside bottom rim of the cage before stepping over it. He walked up to MJ, rubbed his forehead on MJ's chin and began sniffing his face, ears, traveling down his body from head to tail, pausing only to sniff extra around each puncture wound and where his sutures were. MJ bent once to lick Cochon's back as he took his tour. Cochon ignored it, traveling a full circle to end where he began.

How sweet, I thought. Then, out of the blue, he batted MJ in the face. Not hard, no claws out, just his paw. If this was a human interaction, I would have interpreted it as, "Snap out of it!" Maybe Cochon meant the same, but I couldn't know. After batting him, he reared back, neck taut, ready to defend himself if needed.

Instead of reacting, MJ bent forward and stretched down, butt in the air, and meowed, then gave Cochon's head a couple licks with his rough tongue and stepped to the water bowl to drink. Doc nudged me and nodded, looking at the food in my hand.

"MJ, time to eat," I told him, setting his small bowl of leftovers down. Cochon was like a sphynx, watching as MJ sniffed, licked, then relaxed into a crouch as he began to slowly eat. I looked over at Doc. He nodded, grinning, and pointed to a side door.

I followed him into his spacious and comfortable living room, my eye immediately drawn to a large rug hanging between tall bookshelves. I could tell it was created by a Two Grey Hills weaver, the weft so tight it looked like a tapestry. It was exquisite. He kept walking toward the French doors that opened onto a patio dappled in shade. Next to the door on the right was a *nicho* in the wall that displayed a Navajo pot. It was decorated with *Ye'i*, the Navajo spirit deities that taught "The People" to live in harmony with the universe. *How fitting*, I thought, *to have that reminder in this place of healing.*

His home was so richly inviting, I felt I could sit in just that one room forever and not run out of things to look at, think about, read, and admire. Reluctantly, I followed him outside.

"Have a seat and I'll be right back," he said, nodding to a table in the shade. It was a small yard, part emerald-green grass with a large tree, and part xeriscape filled with drought-hardy plants. On the tree side was a rectangular gazebo with grass forming a natural floor. Inside was a splashing water fountain, tree stumps to sit on, and several larger rocks that formed a kind of cave in the back. A roof covered the back half over the little cave and waterfall. By the entrance was the tree that provided shade for the gazebo and the table where I sat down. Then I realized... this odd-looking thing wasn't a gazebo; it was an outdoor kennel.

He returned and handed me a tall glass of cold lemonade with pieces of pulp from the lemon and a couple seeds sitting on the bottom. I thanked him and we sat quiet for a minute, sipping the perfect drink for a summer day.

"Thank you for bringing Cochon and lunch for MJ," he said and leaned forward. "I've seen some very astounding things since I started practicing medicine almost sixty years ago. Western medicine works at its best when used sparingly and with respect..." He paused and smiled. "That's a conversation for another time. But there's an ingredient needed for healing that's often overlooked. When overlooked, sometimes patients die too soon. And I don't want that to happen to MJ. That's why I wanted Cochon here today, to see if he could stimulate MJ's vital force.

"I'm looking for his unique medicine. Modern medicine has cut living things into a pie, so we only see our own slice, or specialty. For example, if someone has a heart attack, we treat the heart. What about the spirit? Forgotten is the mind, what they eat, how they live their days. No one asks about the stressors in their life or what keeps them up at night. And if by some miracle we doctors ask or the patient speaks up, then we send them to someone else to talk to, all the while failing to link the physical with the mental and emotional bodies. We won't be able to truly facilitate healing until medicine is no longer piecemeal.

"The challenge is that most medical doctors—no matter their specialty—aren't trained to address the things that prevent humans and animals from being whole. We weren't trained to be counselors or spiritual guides.

"The other challenge is that the counselors and spiritual guides and others—the bodyworkers, acupuncturists, and workers with energy—are most needed to facilitate lasting healing. Thank heavens we have excellent people offering a more comprehensive approach to people and animals." He shook his head. "But they're the unsung heroes that insurance doesn't cover." He uncrossed his legs and turned to fully face me.

"It's as simple as this: I've had a strong feeling that if I continue to only treat MJ's body, without considering the totality of who he is, he will die. At the very least, he will lose something of intrinsic value and simply..." He paused, searching for the right word. "...fade. Having his wounds heal isn't enough. Already, they're healing a bit slower than would be normal for his body. It's time for a different medicine."

I stared at him. "And *that's* why Cochon is here. He's the medicine."

He nodded. "Think about it: MJ woke up, a stranger in a strange land, as Robert Heinlein might have said. His new environment was a steel prison. His body was in pain, his mind confused, his spirit alone. He awoke with nothing to relate to; no outdoor sights, sounds, smells, feels, no grass under his feet or muscles easily moving. He was displaced into a whole new world of unfamiliarity." He paused, looking down at his hands, then up into my eyes. "Did you ever read *Stranger in a Strange Land?*"

"I did. A long time ago."

"Then I'll use another idea from it: 'sharing water.' In the book, you probably remember that life-giving water was so scarce that sharing it was an act of love. The two that shared it became 'Water Brothers,' a commitment of trust, support, and protection for life," he said.

"I've done some sleuthing over the last couple days. MJ's probably been alone except for the first four or five months of his life. Seems he was part of a barn litter on Barry and Sissy Mackland's farm over fourteen years ago. They had all the kittens spayed and neutered because they wanted them around as mousers for the barn and outside buildings. Then the black one disappeared. We think that was MJ. He fits the profile: all black, teeth that show him about fourteen, and he's been neutered."

I grinned. "Wow, MJ has a real history." Doc was a regular Sherlock Holmes.

Doc continued, "Over those years, he became a creature of survival, enduring weather, thirst, hunger, cat fights, being attacked by other animals, and a solitary life. Then he met Cochon. We'll never know what cosmic alchemy had to exist for those two to be drawn together. What are the odds? An underweight, mute cat, stunted from birth, and a ferocious, feral one. What are the odds that they would not only meet but be inexplicably drawn to each other... so *powerfully* that each would change in order to make room for the other? I can't begin to imagine what this has done for both of them."

I nodded. "It's certainly changed Cochon. After you called, I realized his yells weren't from pain. They were a demand. He's nearly lived at our mailbox since you drove away. When he wasn't watching the road, he was inside pacing back and forth, over and over. Then this morning, he screamed and got into the carrier. I *knew.* I knew he wanted me to take him to where MJ was. Don't laugh, but I knew MJ had somehow called him. Does that sound crazy?"

Doc shook his head. "No, it doesn't. Sometimes we have a gut feeling or an intuition or a glimpse of what's beyond the veil we live behind. For a moment, things become suddenly clear and make sense. I'm glad you listened to what you instinctively knew. I felt something too, and I knew that if he wouldn't eat or drink, if he continued to languish, medicine would only work for a while, and we could lose him.

"When he awoke, even though his body was strong enough to heal, he was without his Water Brother. If I can use a human term, I think he was heartsick." He paused. "*Until* Cochon showed up today," he added. "Now look, he's eating. That's a start. Let's see what happens."

Doc stood up and stretched his back. "I think those two are connected in some beautiful way we may never understand."

Just then the phone rang, and he quickly stepped into the living room. When he returned, he walked straight to what I had decided would be called the Cat Condo and patted its sturdy wooden corner. "If things go as I think they may, I'm transferring MJ to his outdoor house tomorrow. Can you bring Cochon back in the morning around nine?"

"Of course. Want me to bring more food?"

He grinned wide. "I've been cooking today, so we'll be fine for a bit, but thank you. And even though I could continue this conversation for quite a while, that call was from one of Dr. Beaumont's patients. He's not in until noon today, so I'm on call."

We left the beautiful setting and returned to the kennel area. Cochon and MJ were lying on their sides, watching us. I bent down and stepped in, reaching out to rub MJ's head. "Okay, fella, time for Cochon to go home, but we'll be back in the morning." The food bowl was empty. "Good job, buddy," I told him. Then I turned to Cochon. "Okay, Cush, time to go home." I guided him into his carrier without resistance.

Doc grabbed his traveling case, and we walked outside to our cars. "See you tomorrow!" he called as he got into his Travelall. I put Cochon in the front seat and Doc and I waved to each other as he drove away.

Deidre was waiting at the window when we pulled into the driveway. I set the carrier on the ground and opened the door so he could walk with me to our front door. He ran. Inside, Deidre sniffed him all over to get the story of where he'd been. They wound around each other, greeting and exchanging messages. I picked Deidre up, who licked my cheek as I kissed and snuggled. We were all glad to see each other. To express their joy, they chased and tumbled, wearing themselves out in an energetic round of hide-and-go-seek.

Later, both cats cuddled next to me on the couch as I watched *Northern Exposure* on TV. After it was over, I turned off the television and thought about what I'd witnessed. The tables had turned. Cochon had taken the lead today. I had wished I could do more for that big black cat after all he had done for him. Then, today, Cochon showed up. Because life is about showing up. Because they were Water Brothers.

After the evening news, I clicked off the set and watched them sleep, turn, and rearrange themselves. And as animals and people have done since the beginning of time, each reached out every once in a while to touch the other lightly... as if to say, "Just making sure you're here."

16

Synchronicity

"Synchronicity is an ever-present reality
for those who have eyes to see."
– Carl Jung

The cats woke me before first light with voices that announced, in no uncertain terms, it was time for breakfast. I put on a long, thick sweater, hit the brew button, and closed the kitchen window. Even though it was the last week in August, the usual drop of thirty degrees at night felt colder this morning; a hint of fall to come.

I put down their food and stepped outside in pajamas, my sweater, and slippers. I watched the shadows form, lengthen, then disappear as I sipped my coffee, listening to the sounds of song-birds, the caw of a crow, and Emma's distant muted voice floating on the still air of the morning as she cooed, "chick-chick-chick-chick." Two hens (named Minnie and Potato by the local children) were the last of her original brood, now both so old that fresh eggs were a rarity. Minnie and the dubiously named Potato were tended lovingly by Gus and Emma both.

I thought of MJ. Did he regress after Cochon left? I was ready to go back with Cochon and see what had transpired overnight. I looked at my watch. I had time to run out for honey and eggs before heading to Doc's.

Twenty minutes later, I pulled up at Carol and Dave's. Everyone called her "The Egg Lady." Her chickens ran free on her one-acre plot, foraging on native grasses, corn, and grains. The eggs were so fresh, the bright golden-yellow yolks stood up plump and the whites formed a perfect opaque island around them. I loved Carol's eggs. She put them and an extra package in a cloth bag I'd handed her. "Dave went fishin' up in the Jemez, caught us a bunch of trout. I put a nice one in there for you and your cats. It's cleaned and the bones are out. I also have some for MJ that I'll give to Doc later."

I stared at her. "How in the world did you know about MJ?"

"I took Doc eggs and some onions from the garden this morning and he was out back, hammering on that old kennel. I told him about Dave's mess of trout and invited him for dinner tonight. If he didn't have any patients, that is. He said he just had MJ—I guess that's his name, now—who'd been hurt and was recuperating just fine."

She looked at me. "We all know that ugly cat, you know. He killed one of my chickens before we put the fence up and started shooing them in at night. I don't bear a grudge; he was just doing what God put him here to do. He's darn good at it too... gotta admire him for that." I thought of Jake's and my discussion of not condemning or interfering with an animal's nature, and how Carol seemed to know that instinctively.

I handed her a dollar for the eggs. "Let me give you extra for the trout. A little contribution toward some more fat worms for Dave," I said, grinning. I heard he was quite the angler.

She was shooing me with her hands before I finished talking. "Out with you. Dave doesn't go over limit, but he gets slap-happy when he gets out in the rushing water under the Ponderosas in all that rarified mountain air. He brings home way more than we can ever eat or freeze. You go on."

I gave her a little hug. "Would you mind terribly if I also gave this fish to Doc for MJ? I don't mind donating it to the cause—MJ's a big eater, Carol. But I also don't want your feelings hurt."

She laughed at me, "Don't you dare give it to Doc. You enjoy that fish yourself. I'll be sending plenty extra for that beat up old cat home with Doc tonight. We're having a trout banquet. It's the least we can do after he tried so hard to save Kipper's life." I heard a slight catch in her voice. "Oh, of course," she said, suddenly flustered. "You didn't know our Kip. He was the best dog. A little Bichon Frise that loved the world and the world loved him. Dave says he was more human than a lot of humans he knows." She laughed again and ran the side of her finger under one eye.

"Has he been gone long?" I asked.

"No, just a couple months. But that Doc. He slept on our couch the last two nights so he could be there if Kip needed a shot or IV. He had cancer, then surgery, did well for a while, then it came back. I think Kip was tired."

"I'm so sorry, Carol. You didn't say a word when I came for eggs. And I never even saw Kip," I said.

"Well, he was old and he'd lost the use of his back legs, so Dave made him a little scooter thing to help him get around. It took two of us to lift him and the cart outdoors, so he wasn't outside in the daytime unless it was the weekend." She picked up a tissue and blew her nose.

I reached out and squeezed her hand. "He sounds like a champ. How old was he?"

She grinned a huge smile. "Almost twenty! Can you believe that? And for the last five years, he ran around in his Kipmobile, little front legs flying, back legs held up by his scooter with wheels. Ugly contraption, but it worked perfect for that little bundle of love. He was without back legs and never complained. Just adapted and kept doing what he did best: bringing happiness to everyone. He was like our child, even though we've got three human ones of our own." She paused. "Oh, boy, is he missed." She dabbed at her upper lip, then straightened her spine and lifted her chin. "But life goes on, right? And Kip never missed an opportunity to bring joy to another human or animal. What a teacher he was! Dave and I decided we'd pick up the mantle for Kip and try to do the same."

As I left with fish and eggs beside me, I was touched by the depth of feeling she had for her little dog. Yet was it any different than the way others felt, including myself? I turned down another street, pulling in at the beekeepers. I picked up a quart jar of local honey—my favorite kind, unheated with little bits of honeycomb floating in the liquid gold. I put my two dollars in the can on the counter of their tiny, open-air stand and waved at Mr. Weatherby out in the field at the hives. Errands done, I headed home. It was almost eight.

I put away the eggs and fish, got Cochon in the carrier, and left Deidre after lots of petting and reassurances that we'd be back soon. She looked sideways at me as if to say, "You *really* think I'm buying that?" and jumped onto the deep windowsill to watch us go. Cochon and I were at Doc's before nine. He met us at the car. "Good morning! Come see what we've got going on out back." He was in his usual high spirits as he offered to carry Cochon. I followed him around the corner, past the office entrance and to the back of the house. It was a glorious morning, tiny wisps of cottony cirrus clouds lazily posing in a deep blue sky.

Grinning, he stopped at the Cat Condo. Inside sat MJ, copper eyes shining as he looked up from where he sat on one of the wide, smooth rocks. "MJ, look at you in your new digs!" I laughed. He meowed in his raggedy voice and Cochon answered, suddenly moving around inside the carrier and scratching the vinal floor.

"Go ahead," Doc said as he handed the carrier to me. I went inside and set it on the grass. MJ hopped down and approached but kept his distance as I opened the little door. Cochon walked out into the grass, sniffed the ground, then the air, his nose taking stock.

I retreated to the table where Doc had sat down, two cups of hot coffee waiting. Then, we watched as the Water Brothers relaxed into each other. Cochon first checked out the whole perimeter, crawled into and out of the little cave, sniffed the water fountain, then jumped up on one stump and then the other. Doc had also put a slim plank of barked wood down and Cochon stepped onto it to scratch as he trimmed his nails.

MJ watched quietly, then joined him at the other end of the plank and scratched, deeply and long, as if he hadn't shed his worn, older claws in a month of Sundays. Cochon stepped off lightly and then spurted across the grass, turned, and ran again in the opposite direction. He jumped onto the top of the cave rocks, leaped down, ran to the other end, then ran straight into MJ and tumbled him onto his side. Then it was MJ's turn to tumble him back, jump onto the rocks and run around the grass. He laid down on his side and Cochon did the same. And their mirroring began, just as they did at home... one closed a paw and the other one did too... one stretched overhead and the other did the same. I imagined it would be as if I looked in a mirror and my image did everything that I did. Only it wasn't me.

"That's interesting," Doc commented as he watched.

"They've been doing that since they met. It seems like a bonding ritual," I told him.

He looked surprised. "That's exactly what I was thinking." After a few minutes, he spoke up again. "It could also be some form of communication we don't understand, a way of sharing inform-ation." Then he shook his head. "I just don't know, but it's fascinating."

At ease, I sipped my cooling coffee and watched them napping, ears attuned to the slightest sounds. "How did he do alone last night?"

"Fine. But he turned quiet again and slept a lot. I moved a lamp and easy chair from a spare bedroom into the kennel area and spent the afternoon reading, giving the floor a good scrub, washed the windows and read some more. I got up once during the night and he was sitting up, absolutely still, with his eyes closed. He didn't move a muscle when I entered. It was eerie. I'm not sure what he was doing."

"Hmm," I said, "maybe he was meditating." Doc looked at me and then we both started laughing.

"MJ, the Buddha Cat!" He continued to chuckle, then turned to me. "Tell me more about this change you've seen in Cochon."

"Well, he was a throwaway in a dumpster, the only one alive of six. When I took him to the vet's that afternoon, she said he looked to be about seven or eight weeks old. But he was so tiny, and he didn't grow much. His adult weight was around six pounds. The hardest thing to get used to was his lack of talking. He didn't even purr or hiss or growl. Nothing. He was incredibly timid, frightened of everything in the world except Deidre and me.

"Until his recent transformation, he had never been around another cat or human. He created an ecosystem to support his fears—drawers, cupboards, closets, under furniture." I let out a big sigh. "Deidre and I grew to live with it. I guess we coddled him too. If someone showed up, I wouldn't open the door until I knew he had hidden himself. If a cat meowed outside the window, I'd close the window so it wouldn't make him run under the bed. Deidre would show up if he was scared and groom him until he had calmed down." I shrugged and shook my head.

"When did he start growing and talking?" Doc asked, interest written all over his face.

"When MJ showed up last Thanksgiving. Instead of hiding, Cochon sat in the windowsill and watched him. Then he'd rub against the glass as if he were greeting MJ. *Totally* out of character. Afterwards, even if he was asleep, somehow he knew MJ was there and he'd wake up and run to the window.

"One day this spring, I let my two out, thinking MJ wasn't coming. He surprised us. Cochon waited on the deck. Normally, if someone even slammed a car door three houses down, he was gone and later I'd find him asleep in a closet. Not this time. He left the deck and walked in grass for the first time and met him halfway, then back to the deck. Then MJ joined us. No touching or sniffing. Just MJ eating, Cochon watching, then both lying down to do their body mirroring for the first time. I think I may have subconsciously noticed Cochon was growing a little, but I ignored it. It happened so slowly.

"A week later MJ challenged him to play, but Cochon wouldn't. Then the day came when he finally left the deck. They played, ran, jumped, even climbed trees. He was this little, timid guy who was suddenly possessed by a tiger." Doc and I both grinned at that. "Next thing, he meowed, and purred, growled, and hissed. Then he stayed out overnight with MJ.

"And from that time on, they've been almost inseparable. And Cochon keeps growing. Not just his body, but his character. He's a different cat—confident, assured. He seems comfortable in his own skin for the first time." I paused. "Do you know what's happening?"

Doc just stared at the two cats, sleeping in the quiet of the morning. "I wish I did because it's probably unprecedented. There are things over the years that I've put in a box called 'Miracles'—cancers disappearing without treatment, wounds healing almost overnight, organs that quit and started again, babies born against all odds. I'll have to put this into the Miracle Box.

"Keep in mind, however, that I'm not a vet. I'm a people doctor. But I've never heard of an adult cat having a growth spurt of this magnitude. Brother Jim might have seen or heard of it. Not for the first time, I wish he was here." A look of wistfulness flickered over his face, then was gone.

We sat in the quiet for a few moments. I thought of my own siblings. I knew it would break my heart if one of them died. But already, Doc had moved on from that past moment into this present one. "Did you see his wounds? They look very good today. I attribute that to Cochon's presence and MJ knowing both of you are still in his world."

"How long will he be here?"

"Maybe a couple weeks for the tissue to fully knit, give or take. I want to make sure it stays clean and he doesn't engage in any activity that rips the sutures or opens those puncture wounds back up."

I looked at the Cat Condo and turned to him. "You aren't afraid he'll climb the screen or stretch too high and tear his stitches? He's quite athletic."

Doc grinned. "I replaced all the screening with a special type that he can't get his nails into. He can't climb *or* get caught in it. He's land-bound for the next two weeks. Jim built that outdoor kennel. We didn't have the right screening back then, so it was used mostly for dogs." His eyes gave the kennel a full once-over. "You would have liked my brother. Very smart and wise about any animal that ever lived. But not about people. He couldn't stand most of 'em."

Doc refilled our coffee cups from a carafe and we talked a while longer. Then he had patients to see—two-legged and four-legged. "When shall I pick up Cochon? Or do you want him to spend the night?"

He hesitated. "Would you be okay with that?"

I shrugged. "If it helps MJ and Cochon is willing."

I entered the Condo and sat on one of the wooden stumps. It was warm from the dappled sun. The fresh wood smell was rich and aromatic. I pulled the carrier to me, opened the door, and turned it around to face Cochon.

"You can stay or come home. It's your choice, Cush." He glanced at the carrier, then at me, then walked over to rub against my calves. I massaged his head, shoulders, and back, smoothing him from his head to the tip of his tail. He laid down and I continued stroking—thighs, tummy, and then back to his head. "Whatcha think?" I whispered. He lay there, totally relaxed, the slight breeze ruffling his long fur like a wheat field undulated by a gentle wind. I waited a couple minutes, then stood up. I had my answer.

I arrived home to find a plastic bag hung on the doorknob and a note from Emma inside with homemade oatmeal cookies. "Miss you!" was all it said. It was on pink paper with white flowers in the corner. The bottom of the sheet was scalloped. It couldn't have been more feminine. It made me realize there were depths I hadn't seen.

Emma was from Arkansas, as was Gus. She was a tall woman, about 5'10 she told me, and she was what people might call "big-boned." She had broad shoulders and hips, her hands were large, she wore a size eleven shoe, and a sixteen to eighteen dress, depending on the brand. She didn't look like she carried extra weight, she just looked solid.

She told me her father called her "sturdy." She also told me she hated the word. What young girl in high school wants to be thought of as sturdy? She wore no makeup except the occasional lipstick when she "dressed up." Her hair was short, medium brown with a few grey ones on top, rather amazing for a woman in her seventies. She was strong of character, as well as body.

Emma's physical glory was her face. It was round and happy with beautiful skin and laugh lines around her eyes and mouth. It was rare to see her with anything less than a grin on her lips. She had large, rich brown eyes that pulled you in for a deeper look. They were inviting when she laughed, as if they were daring you to join in and lighten up. They were a warm hug when you were hurting. They told the story of her heart.

She mostly wore dresses and sensible shoes, another term she didn't like. I only saw her in one pantsuit that had a fancy jacket. She never wore jeans. Over her dresses she wore a full apron that looked like the front half of a dress. I remembered both my grandmothers wore them when I was little. It had a loop to go around your neck, a tie in the back, and a big pocket in front. The pocket held her necessities: close-up glasses and a hanky. It could also hold string beans from the garden, the occasional egg from Minnie or Potato, and the day's mail.

She was one of the most intelligent women I knew, openly curious and perceptive. She worked through problems quickly, could discuss almost anything, and didn't believe something just because someone said it or wrote it. She got the facts and made up her own mind.

She cared about me, listened intently, asked interesting questions, offered her well-earned wisdom, laughed, challenged me when it was needed and hugged me when it wasn't. She was beautiful inside and that made her even more beautiful outside. She was my friend.

So, I wasn't surprised when she came over almost as soon as I got home. "You've been in and out so much, I wanted to catch you before you took off again." She laughed and hugged me. We sat on the couch and Deidre joined us, moving to Emma's lap for some attention and approval; A&A, as Emma called it.

I brought her up to date on everything that happened, including this strange feeling I'd had of being immersed in a play where I was the supporting cast. She nodded. "I know that feeling. The pastor talked about it one Sunday and called it a fancy word: synchronicity. Big word for when somethin' seems like a coincidence or chance, but it's more like a postcard from life. It writes to you, sayin' you're on the right path and there's gifts a'waitin' for you." And I thought that's exactly what it felt like.

I shared Cochon's strange behavior this morning and the "Water Brothers" idea of Doc's. She had read Heinlein's book and agreed there was something very tender and almost otherworldly about the two cats. I also told her Cochon would spend tonight with MJ at Doc's.

She clapped her hands together. "Oh, wonderful! That MJ will get a good dose of the magic he's created. The love in that little guy will be just what he needs. What a great idea!" Emma asked to go with me in the morning to pick up Cochon, and we made plans for 8:30.

I was glad Cochon was with his friend, though already I was aware of his absence. I could tell Deidre was too. Before Emma had dropped over, I'd picked her up for hugs and she spent extra time sniffing my hands and fingers. I wondered what the smells told her. She also wanted outside right away and stayed on the deck without me for a long while, testing the air, watching, assessing, listening.

That night Deidre was restless. "He'll be home tomorrow," I whispered as I rubbed her ears and face and under her chin, which she extended full-length so I could get every part. I understood. It was their first time apart.

She slept very close that night, spooning against my tummy. When I turned over, she repositioned herself, her warm back pressed to mine. As I drifted back to sleep, a memory surfaced on a stunning moment.

As I'd left the Cat Condo that afternoon, I had just closed the gazebo door when I happened to look up into MJ's piercing copper eyes. Like magnets, they held mine and we looked at and into each other as the moment stilled. Tonight, I realized that if I could have put words to that feeling I had as I met his gaze, it would have been *timeless*.

17

Box of Rocks

*"You can't start the next chapter of your life
if you keep re-reading the last one."*
— Michael McMillian

Emma came over at 8:30am, carrying a covered stock pot. "I
thought Doc might enjoy some biscuits and gravy. I used Shar's
homemade pork sausage she makes whenever they butcher a hog.
You haven't tasted perfection until you've had her sausage," she
said.

I'd heard of Shar and Samuel's small farm between Bosque
Farms and Albuquerque. I also heard they raised their pigs like they
did their kids: with plenty of love, healthy food, sunshine, and fresh
air.

As she put the pot between her feet on the car floor, she told
me she was looking forward to seeing Doc. "It's been a month o'
Sundays since we've had him over to dinner. After Rosalie died, I
think half the town invited him to eat, and he's such good company,
we keep on doin' it." She shook her head, grinning. "My, he's loved

in this little hamlet on the river." I listened, driving slowly down the small back streets that led to Doc's, content to hear her talk and chuckle, a musical sound that harmonized with the soft birdsong in the morning air.

I asked her if she had met Dr. Beaumont yet, Doc's medical replacement downtown at the old office. She told me she'd gotten her yearly checkup from him a couple weeks ago. "He seemed right fine. All business and rules, which is fine. But he doesn't touch you in kindness, look you in the eyes, or listen very well. He gives you the feelin' you're there to listen to *him* because he's the authority—not you, for heaven's sake. How could *you* know what's goin' on in your own body? You're just the person who lives in it!" She laughed at the silliness of it all.

"Maybe they could start teachin' kindness in medical school. Sometimes when folks are sad or don't feel well, just hearin' 'em out helps. Maybe train 'em to quit schedulin' so many people so they have time to listen to what's said... *and* what's not said. Then, teach 'em a patted hand or smoothed back or little hug is as healin' as a pill. Sometimes more." I nodded, thinking the older people in my life had so much to offer, if I kept listening.

At Doc's, we went to the clinic door. It was locked so we continued around the house. He was just leaving the Cat Condo, swabs, gauze, and a bottle of something in hand. "Good morning! Emma, what a treat!" he called to us. "I'll be right back. There's coffee on the table. Help yourself." He went in through the French doors.

Emma set her pot down, then reached in her large sweater pocket and removed three cloth napkins, three forks, and a small ladle. "I come prepared," she laughed, folding the napkins into triangles, and putting a fork on top of each one.

Doc returned, went straight to Emma, and they hugged. "So good to see you!" he said. "Are you well? And Gus?" She assured him they were.

"I brought a little breakfast for us that won't stay hot for long. How about we go back in and get a couple things?" They left, Doc's arm around her shoulder, laughing about something as they disappeared into the house.

I immediately went to the Condo and stepped inside. "Cochon, my sweet boy," I said, going straight to him and picking him up. We nuzzled and I confessed my love for the millionth time, then set him down. Then, I went to MJ and stuck out my finger for him to check. He sniffed it thoroughly then meowed in his gravelly voice. I gently scratched the top of his head as I studied his right shoulder and left haunch, souvenirs from being impaled by the talons of one of nature's great wonders. Each wound looked almost the color of the shaved skin around it. I had a sense that was good.

Two minutes later, they returned with one more coffee mug, three plates, and salt and pepper. I watched as she uncovered the deep pot that held a small crock and a foil-wrapped bundle that held her huge homemade biscuits. She fork-split three of them into halves, carefully putting two halves on each dark-green plate. Then, she removed the crock's lid and ladled out her rich, homemade gravy on each half. The smell of spices and butter made my stomach growl.

"Sawmill gravy, just like my ma used to make. Enjoy!"

Doc reached over and squeezed her hand. "This looks delicious, Emma. Thank you." He reached for my hand, also. "It's a gift to break bread with friends." Emma and I felt the same way as we both squeezed his large, gentle hands in return. The moment felt like a prayer.

We all took our first bites. "The wonderful taste of Shar's sausage." Doc smiled, and Emma nodded, chewing the savory bite. He took another forkful. "And these biscuits are so light. What are they called?"

"They're just buttermilk biscuits, Doc. Nothin' special," she said.

He shook his head. "Let's call them Angel Biscuits—too light to be called anything else." Emma grinned ear-to-ear. I knew she was used to compliments on her cooking, but coming from one she admired so much held weight. I saw her sit up a little bit straighter.

"And I brought extra we're leavin' with you," she said. I could feel her joy in being able to give something to a man who gave so much.

After we'd eaten, he took the plates, utensils, and extra food into his kitchen. He came out a few minutes later with everything washed and dried to go back inside her big pot.

Then, he told us about the Water Brothers. When he looked out the window a few times during the night, they were either sleeping or playing with each other or intently watching something outside. "Evidently, my yard is full of interesting things in the dark," he said. Cochon hadn't wanted much of the type of food MJ ate, so Doc told me he would be hungry when he got home. He'd put a litter box inside and Cochon used it; MJ preferred the dirt in the corner. And this morning, MJ's wounds looked amazingly good.

"They're good for each other," Emma said. "And such a nice little outside place for them to be—a little like what MJ's used to. Didn't Jim build that kennel?"

"He did. I put in different screening and added a water fountain, built a little shallow cave, and added some cut wood stumps and a scratching board. Jim built it, I did the decorating," he told us, smiling.

"I call it the Cat Condo," I told them, and they both laughed.

"Perfect name," Emma said, still watching them. "Could I go in and pet on Cochon?"

Doc hesitated. "Do you mind waiting, Emma? For now, it's better only she and I go in," he said, nodding at me. "And sparingly at that. My sense is that MJ will remain feral. I don't want him to get used to people and lose his keen sense of caution. Not everybody loves cats."

"Good idea, Doc," she said. "I can visit Cochon later. And I haven't had contact with MJ, so you're right—best not to start now."

"I appreciate that, Doc," I said. "When you told me he'd been feral for fourteen years or more, any lingering hope of him moving in with us finally left. My friend, Jake, and I talked about this at length a few months ago. It's been hard to not interfere."

Doc took another sip of his coffee. "Looks like you're doing a perfect job of stepping in right when you're needed," he said. "And let's wait a couple days now before you bring Cochon back. I want to see if MJ continues his progress alone. How about Monday morning?"

"That's good." I looked at Emma, smiling. "And maybe you'll come back too."

"God willin' and the creek don't rise, I'll be here."

I looked at Doc and Emma. "Do you have a few more minutes to talk? I'm working to stay out of the future... catching myself when my mind wants to produce movies. Without so many forays into the scary unknown, I've got a little more energy and a clearer mind. It feels so much better." I reached out and squeezed Emma's hand. "Since we talked, I'm much less anxious. I can't thank you enough, Emma."

"You're welcome, honey. But it wasn't so much my doing. You were just ready to hear it."

"I agree," Doc said. "We seem to only hear what we're ready to hear. Sometimes it takes a large life event for us to drop our defenses and open our ears."

I nodded in agreement. "But what I wanted to hear were your ideas on staying out of the past. It seems a natural next step on the way to learning to be present."

He folded his hands and studied them a minute. We waited. I watched the cats batting a piece of bark around in the Condo, at ease in the quiet morning.

Doc cleared his throat. "I'd like to share a story with you. Only Rosalie and Jim ever heard this. It might bring some light to your question about what to do to stay present and not wander backwards into the past. It will just take a few minutes... I believe it's short but powerful. Would you like to hear it?" We turned to face him directly and murmured our yeses.

Doc Parson's Story

When I was much, much younger, just starting medical school, I was very lost and not well physically. I used to take lunch on a park bench near the university. I had been feeling so rotten I was considering quitting school, which scared me. All I had ever wanted to be since I was a little boy was a doctor. I had brought a sandwich, but as I stared at it, I knew I couldn't eat it. I was losing weight but had no appetite. I was taking a full schedule of pre-med classes and working part time in the library. Things were rough at school, at work, and at home with my father. I'd lost my fiancée to a more well-to-do fellow and felt very alone and very melancholy.

This particular day, an old man walked up to the bench and sat down. He had on a lightly stained but clean white apron and white paper hat. He told me he was a fry cook in a nearby restaurant and pointed across the street and down the block a bit. He looked like he was a hundred years old, except he didn't act that way and his eyes were the clearest blue I'd ever seen.

We each said our hellos and made small talk. Then, he turned to me and said, "That box you drag behind you has gotten awful heavy, son." He said it kindly. Kindly or not, it was such a bazaar thing to say that it crossed my mind the old man might be crazy. I hadn't brought a box. But I decided to humor him. I asked what box he was talking about.

"The box of rocks attached to you by a chain that you drag behind you through your every waking hour. The rocks made of anger, bitterness, and resentment. Rocks made of guilt and regret."

I told him I didn't know what he was talking about. He just smiled. "Yes, you do."

How dare he, a stranger, talk to me this way? I put the sandwich in my pocket and stood up to go, but he reached out and gently touched my arm. I don't know why, but I sat down again.

"You think your father let your mother die. He didn't. She was going to die anyway. He was just a hard man, and cruel." I felt my breath catch and stop, frozen in my chest. How did he know this? He wasn't there. I had never seen him before. How did he know that's exactly what I thought?

"And you think your lady friend left you for another man because he was rich. Also not true, but you're mad at her, and mad at him, because you're hurt and want someone to blame for that hurt. You're also angry that a classmate snitched on you in school when you were young. And you still suffer the guilt about your dog that died when you forgot to tie him up and he was trampled by a neighbor's horse."

I felt as if I would faint. How could this one man know so much about me, things I thought were secret, things no one could possibly know? Instead of fearing him, I wanted to sound angry and demand in my most haughty voice, "How dare you, sir! How dare you eavesdrop on my life and spit it out so carelessly!" But all that came out was a faint whisper, "How dare you..." and the rest was lost in my mouth and never left.

I asked him what he wanted of me.

He said, "I want you to live. But you carry so much anger and resentment, so much guilt, regret, and self-pity. There are so many memories and feelings of disappointment, yes?" I nodded, unable to speak. "Each one is a rock you put into a big box that you tug behind you every day. You hold onto anger about today and still feel it tomorrow. That's another rock. And then comes another and another. It's already a heavy burden you carry at your young age."

He smiled a genuinely warm smile. "We don't want you to be destroyed. We want you healthy and strong of spirit, not just body. You have lots of work to do here. You matter in this world, son." I

167

felt tears coating my eyes. No one had ever said I mattered in the twenty years I had been alive. It moved a boulder off my heart and for a moment I felt loved.

He continued, "You don't let go of the past because it gives you an excuse for your behavior today. 'See what happened to my life because he (or she or they) did this?' Or... 'I am the way I am because *that* happened to me!' Whatever you're dragging around could have happened yesterday or years ago. As long as you hold onto it, you avoid the responsibility of creating your own life. You blame people and events of the past and visit them daily to nurse your wounds—it's *their* fault. Or you hold onto regrets and guilts and beat yourself up." He turned to face me. "Son, if you don't stop, that box will be so heavy one day that you won't be able to get up again."

We talked for a while more about what he called my "Accounts Receivables." Then he left, walked quickly across the street, and entered the restaurant on the corner where he worked. It was called Harriet's. He was called Abel.

⌒∾⌒

Doc looked at us. "It was the strangest experience I've ever had. I met with him almost every day for a month. It changed my life. At night, after school or work, I'd go home and write everything down. I kept notebooks that I've read many times. He encouraged me to experiment with what he shared. He didn't want me to believe *him*—he wanted me to check the ideas out for myself and see what worked and what didn't. He cautioned me to not be a collector of words, but to become a student of Life.

"That first night I went home and did as he suggested, mostly to see what would happen. My first notebook was an old ledger. I wrote people's names down and the bad things they'd done on the 'Accounts' side. All the things I was still nursing from thirty years ago. After all, wasn't I justified in reliving those terrible things that happened? Justified because the person had never made good, never apologized, never asked for forgiveness? In my mind, the past hadn't been settled.

"On the other side was the 'Receivables'—the things they had to do to make it right, or to make it go away inside me, all settled and forgotten. What I discovered was curious. I saw that an apology, an admittance of cruelty, or a million mea culpas wouldn't quite mark the account 'Paid.' I would still remember.

"Second, I admitted what I was feeling—angry, hurt, resentful, afraid, and the like. I was taught to be pretty stoic, so I saw those emotions as ugly feelings to be hidden. Abel offered that there was nothing wrong with anger or resentment or regret as long as I didn't become attached and keep them alive.

"Third, I stopped judging either myself or others. That was the hardest part, I think. I wanted to see the world in black or white— good or bad, right or wrong. It's easier to judge when we don't allow subtleties.

"And last, I asked Life for healing and let it go. Abel warned me to not spy on myself and check to see if it was gone. 'No self-respecting body likes to be spied on,' he said. 'Would you like to be spied on all day? It's irritating.'

"He also said to ask God for this gift only once. After all, the Divine isn't deaf. Then he said to let it go. In God's time, not in my time, it would change."

He paused, his eyes focused on something in his memory. "It was difficult to look at myself, as well as remember all my past slights and angers I still carried about others. It was even harder to admit the anger and disappointment I carried toward myself. There were more than a few tears and some moments of rage. But I began to let go. I didn't *try* to let go; things seemed to fade on their own the more I wrote them down and became aware of them. After a while, I could still remember what I or others had done, but when I remembered, there was very little or no feeling about it. My melancholy lifted, and over time my health returned to a level of vitality I hadn't had since my youth."

"Didn't you have to forgive the people who had hurt you? Or forgive yourself for hurting someone else?" Emma asked.

"No. Abel said we aren't capable of forgiving because we'll always remember. However, he told me that if I ask, God would create forgiveness in my heart." Doc paused and grinned. "I told him that might be hard because I didn't believe in God. I wanted to but didn't know God very well and I couldn't believe in something I didn't know. He told me that was okay because the creative force of the universe probably believed in me.

"So, I asked Life—what you may call Creator or God, Spirit or the Divine—to create forgiveness in my heart, and I thanked it." Doc smiled.

"And?" Emma asked.

"It did. And still does to this day."

She slowly nodded. "Oh my, Doc. I got my own box 'a rocks. I'd be happy to let go of 'em. Lord knows I've tried."

"I carry plenty too," I agreed. I also knew our conversation was coming to an end and I was still struggling to apply this in a more personal way to my own life. "Before we end our talk, would you give more examples of things a person might carry around, more of what you call the 'Accounts Receivable' items?"

He thought a minute. "Well, maybe memories of when we were ignored, dismissed, or forgotten—all nice words for feeling unappreciated. Perhaps we felt mistreated or were lied to. We could have been rejected or criticized and left feeling embarrassed or ashamed. We get resentful or hold a grudge against those who shamed or belittled us. Sometimes we just resent the heck out of the person for being so clueless and inconsiderate." He leaned back and looked at us intently.

"We dredge up things from twenty years ago, or we remember what happened this morning. We go to bed angry or hurt and the next day dawns and we're still thinking about it, rolling it over in our minds. The more we think about it, the angrier or more hurt we get. Our resentment grows. We think we deserve an apology or, at the very least, we need them to change their behavior."

"Shape up and fly right," Emma added.

"Exactly." Doc chuckled. "But if I've determined that the only way I can feel better or be all right is if *you* change, now I'm in trouble. Just that one little thing effectively stops me from being responsible for the only thing in the world I have 100 per cent control over: *how I feel.*

"My mood is my choice, no one else's. How I feel inside is my choice. But if I can't feel better until *you* change, now I have to wait until you change. I may even expend a lot of energy trying to get you to change. I've put you in charge of how I feel.

"But the truth is no one is in charge of how someone feels. No one is so powerful that they can reach inside you and make you feel something. What and how we feel is *always* up to us."

I shook my head, thinking of times I had done these very things as I imagined my own box and its weight. "What about feeling guilty? That's from the past."

"*There's* a couple of doozies: guilt and regret," he said. "All the things we should have done but didn't. Those two never show up without a bullwhip to crack, 'You're to blame; it's all your fault! You're not good enough! You're lacking (or wrong or bad). You failed!' And they repeat themselves. And we believe them. Now the box is *really* heavy.

"Abel said we hold onto the past for one of three reasons: either to justify our behavior, avoid taking responsibility, or to lick our own wounds. Every time we bring up our past and feel bad or beat ourselves up, we reopen the wound. However long we bring that stuff up and feel sorry for ourselves is equal to how long we live with wounds that won't heal. Can you imagine a wound that never heals?"

Emma shifted in her chair and said, "Isn't this just the saddest thing. We feel all hurt inside, we keep feelin' sorry for ourselves, we bring up the sadness and cuddle ourselves with it. You're right. It's a guarantee those wounds'll *never* heal."

Doc nodded and turned to me. "Does that help?"

"It does, Doc." I hesitated to ask, but I did anyway: "Have you left the past behind?"

"Yes. Mainly because I'm selfish." Emma and I looked at each other, eyebrows raised, and then at him. He continued, "I'm selfish because I found out what it feels like to not drag that weight around, and I don't think I can describe how freeing it is. I want to feel this way as much as humanly possible. I'm just fine with giving up my resentments and self-pity in exchange for the clarity and energy I feel."

We sat at the table, talking under a clear blue New Mexico sky for over an hour. I thought of the hurts I nursed from my past marriage. The old Ray Price song, "You Done Me Wrong", passed through my head. There were still angers festering from what people had done or said years ago. All of that was in me. I didn't want it to be a part of my life anymore. I looked at Doc, a little over eighty with the energy of a much younger man. I wondered if letting go of that burden, that heavy box, helped us to not become old before our time.

I looked over at MJ and Cochon again. They were lying on their sides in the shade of the honey locust, resting. I pointed to them. "Maybe those are the true buddhas on earth. Cats and dogs don't hold grudges, have you noticed? They don't have to learn to let go because they don't hold on. They learn from their past, but they don't drag every hurt into their present. They experience life moment by moment. How amazing," I said and looked at them with a new understanding that some of my teachers had been here all along, had I but paid attention.

After I said goodbye to MJ and coaxed Cochon into the carrier, Doc walked us out to the car. Emma asked him why he only spent a month talking to Abel. Doc said that was a strange thing. "One day," he said, "Abel didn't meet me at the bench. I waited fifteen minutes, then finally walked across the street and down to Harriet's. I was concerned that he might be ill and thought I would check on him. I asked a waiter if Abel was cooking today. He sent me to the manager who stared at me in confusion, then said they didn't have any 'Abel' working there. I described him down to the white cap and apron he always wore.

"The manager said he hadn't ever seen anyone matching that description, not even coming in to eat. He said I must have the wrong place. I started to argue and told him I'd watched Abel go in this restaurant every day for a month. My eyes knew what they had seen. Thirty times I'd watched the door with 'Harriet's' on the glass swing open and fall closed. But the manager interrupted and told me in a haughty voice, with dramatic inflection, that *he* was there seven days a week from early morning until after dinner rush, and if *anyone* had seen this man, it would have been *him*. No one like that had ever come through *his* door. 'Our cooks don't even wear caps,' was his final word as he turned on his heel, reaffixed his smile, and welcomed a new patron."

Emma and I didn't talk as we drove back. She helped me get Cochon in the house and then started to walk home. Halfway to her drive, she turned back and faced me. Her face was radiant. "Forgive me for sayin' this, but I'm thankful MJ got hurt and needed Doc. None of this seems like a coincidence. It feels like what we talked about before: synchronicity. It took MJ being injured to bring all this about... hearin' Doc's story, learnin' from him and you and Cochon and MJ. It's all tied together and happenin' for a reason. Do you see?" I nodded, aware we were willing participants in the same story.

She shook her head. "What an utterly generous and magical world we live in." And her smile was bright like a star being born.

18

Oh, it's You!

"Only the strong can afford to be gentle and kind."
– Abel

I loved all the New Mexico seasons. Fall didn't just "arrive"—it thrust itself in, pushing summer out of its way. It was my favorite time of the year, an explosion of color, vibrancy, and change. Everything seemed to say, "Move faster! The time of hibernation is coming."

In the town of Hatch, the self-proclaimed "Chile Capital of the World," bushy chile plants stretched toward the sun as they drank from the Rio Grande and the occasional summer storm. In August and September, to prevent bruising the vegetables, green chiles were harvested as they always had been, by strong hands, arms, and backs. Thousands of forty-pound burlap bags were loaded onto long flatbed trailers headed for grocery store parking lots, farmers markets, and roadside stands all over the state and beyond. It was time to fire up the roasters.

The roasting of green chiles sends a sweet, smoky perfume into the air. The shiny, long green fruit is dumped from its burlap bag into a large steel cylinder cage that rotates over an open flame. The skin chars, imparting a gentle smoky flavor, then falls off through the openings in the cage. From there, the chiles are put into clear plastic bags and sold.

I had traveled with friends to the tiny town of Hatch, located about two and a half hours south of Albuquerque, for the Hatch Chile Festival. We would stand beside the noisy drums with their propane firing and the inedible chile skins popping and blistering. It was a sound of New Mexico. One old man told me he was glad it was mechanized so he didn't have to turn the drum by hand anymore.

In Hatch I'd buy the thicker, meatier green chiles for chile rellenos, and pre-chopped fresh green chiles for everything else. I would also buy a couple long *ristras*: vibrant strands of red peppers strung together to hang as a New Mexico welcome outside my door. As they dried and their beauty began to fade, they moved to their next life as the base of red chile sauce and pure red chile powder.

But this year I stayed home and went alone to the local grocers who had set up their roasting drum outside in the parking lot. I bought extra for Doc who I knew wouldn't issue a bill or take money. At home I hung my new bright-red *ristras*, then went to work cleaning the last of the burnt skins off the whole chiles and putting them into freezer bags. The diced chiles were put by the cupful into smaller ones. I missed taking the beautiful drive south, but I didn't want to leave the cats this year.

Early Monday morning, Emma and I went back to Doc's, Cochon in his carrier, green chiles in a sack, the sun sparkling off the last of the dew on the fields. It had rained overnight, and the land wore its extra water like a diamond-studded, green velvet blanket.

Doc was his usual chipper self, coffee waiting on the patio table. He told us MJ started talking before we even drove up. Cochon did the same. Emma said she thought he was talking to himself. I told her I thought he was talking to MJ, though I doubted they needed meows to do that. I gave Doc a hug, handed him the green chiles, then went to the Cat Condo to open the carrier. Cochon pranced out into the grass to MJ, two wet noses touched in greeting. Smelling and circling and soft head- and body-butting ensued. Then they released the energy of their joy, running, tumbling, then stopping to listen to a rustling bird in the bushes or something in the sky only they could hear.

Doc hugged Emma, then took the chiles to the garage freezer. Returning, he poured coffee and we all sat down. "How did he do over the weekend?" I asked him as I warmed my hands on the mug.

"Quite well, though without Cochon and a world to explore, I think he was a little under stimulated. It won't be long. He's healing beautifully."

Emma grinned. "What good news. It's a testimony to Cochon's and your love." She watched the cats for a moment and then said, "I think love is the real healer. I've seen it do powerful things."

I nodded and Doc smiled, admitting he had seen healing beyond reason because of love. Deep within myself, a little voice whispered, *Isn't this amazing? To start your day with friends who casually mention over coffee that love has the power to heal? How blessed am I?* And I felt like crying with the bounty of it all.

We went on to talk about the rain, the Hatch Chile Festival this coming weekend, the State Fair in mid-September, and the 19th Annual Balloon Fiesta in October. "You probably never heard of them, but the Balloon Fiesta Rock and Glo has one of my favorite musical groups this year called Three Dog Night. I plan on being there," I announced.

"I never heard of 'em, but if you have a tape, I've got a cassette player. I'd like to hear their music," Emma said. "You don't know. I might enjoy it. Leastways, it might be good music to get me up and going to clean house when I need a little boost," she said, laughing. I tried to picture Emma singing along to "Joy to the World," one of their more popular songs... and I could. That was the beauty of Emma.

Doc told us he had a patient coming in a few minutes. It was a quick procedure and wouldn't take very long. Though we didn't hear a car, the cats suddenly sat up straight, ears turned toward the house. "That must be my appointment. Cats are great watch dogs." He grinned. "I'll be back in a few minutes." He walked into the house. We heard talking and another man's voice. Then, a tall, skinny man walked through the French doors.

"Emma!" he yelled.

"Barry Mackland, you old coot!" They hugged. He pulled out a chair and joined us after introducing himself to me. "Whatcha doin' here, Barry? Is Ferrari okay?" Emma asked, concern in her voice.

"'Ferrari, He Who Runs Like the Wind', as Doc calls him, has a little infection on his face. He had one last year but it went away pretty quick." His long, spidery fingers drummed the table. "We've got lots to do today. Going up to the city to drop off a bunch of boxes at that place that takes donations. Sissy's been cleaning house like we're welcoming the Queen of England. I told her—" He stopped and stared at the Cat Condo. "Is that him? Is that that old black cuss that ran away some fourteen years ago?" And suddenly it clicked. This was the man Doc was talking about when he told me about MJ being born at Barry and Sissy Mackland's farm.

"We can't go in the kennel, Barry, but you can go up to the door if you want to see him better," I told him. Barry was what some would call a 'tall drink of water'—I guessed him at 6'5 or so and his stride was long. He reached the door in four easy steps and just stood there, looking, quiet. Then he returned to the table and sat again.

"He's one ugly son of a gun. Wonder what happened to that ear. Something took a bite out of it. Makes him look like he's not all the way made," he said, frowning as he studied MJ. "And that line of skin missing on his front leg, a chunk of fur missing on his cheek, and now Doc's shaved him to a fare-thee-well. He's had a hard life, that one. But damn if he isn't still here." His eyes wondered how that had happened.

Emma patted his arm, "Well, Barry, he had a good beginnin' with you and Sissy, didn't he? How are his siblings doing?"

Barry shook his head. "Only one left. They were good mousers for a number of years, then somethin' got in the barn and killed a couple. Another one got sick and died. The last one—Lazy we named her 'cause as a kitten she slept a lot—has lived up to her name. That was before Doc and I talked about people and animals growing into their names, so be careful what you name 'em." He looked at us, nodding his head, as if making sure we were hearing him. He stretched his long legs out to the side and leaned back, looking around. "Doc's got him a real nice place here... mighty peaceful." Emma agreed and they changed the subject to the upcoming fair.

I heard a bark from inside, which Barry and Emma ignored. I was looking forward to finally meeting the famous Ferrari I'd heard so many times barking in Barry's field. Ferraris were lightning-fast cars, so I imagined a sleek Greyhound or maybe a graceful Whippet—dogs that ran like the wind, puppies that would grow to be fleet of foot.

Another bark and Doc walked out, holding and tugging lightly on a red leash. "Come on, Ferrari, He Who Runs Like the Wind." To my utter surprise, out walked a thick, squat, short-legged, fawn-colored Bulldog. As soon as the dog saw Barry, he went wild, barking, snuffling, and whining as Doc unhooked the leash.

Barry turned in his chair, grinned wide enough to show some molars, and called, "*There* he is! It's *You!*" as if he hadn't seen him in years. Ferrari ran to him, making ecstatic grunting and snuffling sounds as he put his front paws on Barry's knees, wagging his little stub of a tail so hard his whole hind end wagged. Barry picked him up and hugged him, talking to him like they had so much to catch up on. "I've missed you, you beautiful boy! How's that face doing? Doc make it all better? Don't you look handsome!" He checked

Ferrari's left cheek, touching it lightly. "Looks like it has some salve on it, that right, Doc?"

Doc sat down with us. "It was infected, but lightly. He'll be fine. You keep cleaning it with the antibacterial soap I've put in a bag for you and apply the balm with a Q-tip. Drop by in a week and I'll take a look." He reached out and smoothed Ferrari's head. "You're quite something, you know that?" he said to the drooling dog. And Ferrari whined and snuffled his agreement, his backend going into high gear all over again.

"Well, ladies and gentleman, time for us to go. He Who Runs Like The Wind and I have miles to go before we sleep. Isn't that right, my friend?" He kissed the top of Ferrari's head, then set him down. Doc walked them to Barry's car.

When he returned, I had to ask. "'Ferrari', Doc? I understand growing into your name, but no bulldog will ever run like a greyhound, let alone a Ferrari. How can a stubby-legged pup that sounds like he has asthma run like the wind?"

Doc just grinned. "We don't have to *look* like our names, just grow character-wise into their potential. We can only hope to take the qualities of our names and *feel* like them. Bulldogs are prone to all kinds of problems: hips, breathing, skin, and a tendency to get fat. But if his heart embodies the character of one of the fastest, sleekest, strongest automobiles made, and if Sissy and Barry treated him that way, I figured he'd have a better go at life than if they named him 'Pudge'... Which was what they wanted to name him because he was such a fat puppy."

Doc told us Barry took him out every few days and played frisbee with him, mindful to throw low to the ground. True to his name, at almost eight years old, Ferrari was still very fast and a great frisbee catcher. He loved running, though he tuckered out sooner than later. Doc said all that exercise kept him trim and muscular. "Barry told me if they hadn't named him Ferrari, he would have coddled him and ended up with an overweight, lazy lap dog."

"What was so amazing was how utterly ecstatic that dog was to see Barry, and they'd been separated for what? All of ten minutes? And it was mutual," Emma said. "What an expression of love. I can't think of a human that wouldn't give their eye teeth to have someone say, 'Oh, it's *you!*' to them once in a while when they come home."

"Might save a few marriages," Doc chuckled, "and it doesn't take much energy to say."

"A&A," Emma said. "Attention and approval. How did you say it, Doc?"

"We need attention to survive and approval to thrive." He looked at the cats. "I've seen people change, feel better, even be healed of diverse things because they received some A&A. I've seen relationships mend, and hearts mend, and people blossom into more than they thought possible. I think perhaps MJ and Cochon have given this to each other, especially the thriving part."

I looked into the Cat Condo and Cochon was resting while MJ watched something attentively in the tree. "Maybe MJ's attention and approval have been a factor in Cochon's growth spurt. But it still doesn't make sense, because he always had tons of A&A from Deidre and I." I heard myself and then remembered Emma's and my conversation on this very thing. So easily I had forgotten.

Emma squeezed my hand briefly. She was too classy to remind me that she'd cleared this up for me one time before. "Of course he has. But maybe your little guy needed some pushin' and challengin'. Not all attention is the same. MJ seems to give somethin' rare that affects both body *and* spirit."

"Powerful stuff," Doc added.

I looked at them both. "You two are so patient. I know you've both said this already to me in different ways. I'm still trying to make sense of all of this. I appreciate the repetition." I smiled while feeling a little embarrassed.

"There's no problem in retellin' and no shame in rehearin'," Emma said. "All the meaningful things bear repeatin'. Repetition is a good thing. And when I say somethin' twice or more to Gus or you or Doc, I get to hear it one more time and gain a better understandin'. It's for me as much as for you."

"One thing we all know for sure," Doc said, "is that whatever is happening with these two cats is unusual with parts that are both incomprehensible and magical. In my own life, if I didn't pay close attention when these events came along, I would have lost what could have been a great gift. That makes me pay extra attention to what unfolds with these two."

"Is that the way you felt when you were with Abel?" I asked him. "Like you needed to pay close attention because it was so unusual?" He nodded. "I thought of your story and worked some over the weekend on writing down things to release." I paused and grinned. "Still working on it and probably will be for a bit. But I wanted to ask you a question."

"Of course, Anything," he said.

"Okay, then of all the things you talked about, all the wisdom he gave you, what stands out as the one thing you remember most?"

Doc was quiet as he looked far off, perhaps seeing the Manzanos in the distance. Perhaps looking inward. I was still, content to Wait with a capital "W". Then, he looked over at us and said:

"Only the strong can afford to be gentle and kind."

That was all he said.

On the way home, Emma told me when he quoted that one line, something shifted inside, making her see people and their behaviors a little differently, herself included. She called it a change in perspective. "That's a sentence I'm going to think on for a while," she told me.

But I didn't think of it in terms of the people I knew or of myself. I thought of MJ, how powerful he was, how I'd been told he chased attacking dogs, drove off a coyote, and had fought a Great Horned Owl. He was a warrior. Yet, it was his gentleness and kindness that had attracted us. It was his gentleness and kindness that was healing Cochon. That was MJ's true strength. Perhaps it was the true strength in all of us.

19

The Knower Knows

"When we share our lives with animals,
our spiritual paths intertwine."
– Kathleen Prasad

Two nights later, I awoke from a dream. In it, I walked into the living room at my parents' home and my sister was there. She grinned and said something, but I couldn't hear her. I told her to speak up, and I could tell by her demeanor that she did and said something again as she grinned. I still couldn't hear her. She kept talking and gesticulating in her usual way. It was like having the television on, but muted. I became frustrated and told her again in a loud voice, "I can't hear you!" and she answered but there was still no sound. For some unknown reason, it was frightening, and I woke up with a start.

I don't know why this bothered me so much. I turned over and looked at the clock. It was almost 4am. Deidre and Cochon shifted as I turned, then went back to their own cat dreams. I quietly got out of bed and put on a robe. September had arrived and instead of the thrill I had been feeling in anticipation of the many festivities and changes that accompanied cooler weather, this morning I felt an almost imperceptible sense of foreboding.

I got a glass of water, hit the brew button for coffee, and went to the family room. As I sat, draped under a blanket, staring into the flat, pre-dawn blackness, the question that came to me was, "Who am I not hearing?"

I'd had countless dreams in my life. Most were random leftover thoughts, like Scrooge's assessment of Marley's ghost, "You may be an undigested bit of beef, a blot of mustard, a crumb of cheese..." But some I called "events," experiences so vivid that not only did I know I was asleep in my bed, but I also knew I was someplace else where I was being given information that brought color to the muted understanding of my life. These were different and I paid attention. The dream that woke me was an event, but this time I didn't understand the message.

I walked quietly into the kitchen and poured a cup of coffee, looking out the window over the sink. All I saw was the reflection of the orange brew button in the glass. *Who am I not hearing?* I thought of Deidre, MJ, and Cochon... of Emma and Gus, Carlita, of Doc, Jake, Maureen, Barry, and Ferrari. Even Carol the Egg Lady and her little Kip, who left his message behind to be passed on by those he loved. I went back to the couch and settled under the blanket, seeing each face in my mind's eye.

I had learned from all of them. They had been generous in sharing their wisdom, not only their time and kindness. I had listened well, writing down conversations and what I had learned, filling several notebooks. At that moment, I couldn't feel more thankful to live here in this special place.

And yet I was still no closer to understanding who I wasn't listening to.

As I looked into the night, the first hint of light outlined the top of the Manzano Mountains. Deidre joined me, hopped onto my lap, and kneaded the blanket—"making bread," my mother called it—

as she greeted me with her strong purr. "Good morning, beauty," I purred back. Then she hopped down and meowed. Breakfast time.

Cochon was also up, and I fed them both. When they wanted out, I joined them on the deck to watch the pink and peach sprays of morning light against a cloudless sky. They were content to listen, smell, and watch, ever alert. Today, Cochon would be dropped off at Doc's again to spend the day with MJ. Emma couldn't come, so I would be going alone, hopefully for more conversation.

A couple hours later, Cochon and I left, Deidre watching us from the window. I looked forward to having MJ back and not leaving her behind. I wanted Cochon there to help MJ heal, but I could tell Deidre had had about enough of this being alone stuff.

Cochon was in high spirits as we pulled in. There was a car in the drive and the clinic door was locked, so I walked around back to the Condo where MJ was waiting by the door, greeting me with his signature ragged meow. I lifted Cochon out of his carrier, opened the door, and scooched him inside. They went through their greeting stage of sniffing heads, ears, behinds, and lightly leaning into each other, circling, and then a game of chase began. It wasn't that big an area, but they ran it like an obstacle course—stump to corner, jumping to the top of the cave, down on the grass, over to the opposite corner, back to the other stump. I walked over to Doc's fence, an adobe wall, and leaned against it, looking out over the field. Birds tittered and a great hawk flew overhead.

Shortly I heard voices, a door close, and out came Doc with a pot of coffee and two mugs. "Good morning! Do you have time for a cup?" he asked. I said I did, and as he poured, he told me about cleaning MJ's wounds this morning. "If I didn't know better, I would think they were two weeks old, not a week. He may come back sooner than I thought. The hair is even starting to grow back. He seems to be quite the healer," he said, a tinge of admiration in his voice.

As we talked, I thought of the dream I had and told him about it. "I've had realistic dreams before, so real I would swear I had been in the dream's house or room or field just moments before I woke up. In the past, this type of dream made sense and I understood the message. But not this time. The only thing that keeps popping up is the question, 'Who am I not listening to?' I've thought of everyone I know, and I can't think of anyone I'm not hearing. Unless I'm fooling myself."

Doc nodded and was quiet a moment, seemingly lost in thought. Then he looked up. "A long while ago, I spent a lot of time studying dreams. I was treating a man who had what we used to call 'night terrors,' and I didn't know a thing about them. As I read, I became fascinated. There are many opinions on what to think about dreams. I've found what works best for me is to see each person in the dream as myself. Ninety-nine percent of the time, I am the creator of the dream. As a possibility, how would seeing your sister as yourself make a difference?"

I grinned. "Well, I think it would mean that a part of me is trying to tell me something and I'm not listening."

Doc nodded. "Is that possible?"

"Yes. I have tuned out ideas and thoughts, warnings and intuitions, that in hindsight were spot on. I know feeling regret is a waste of time, but I have regretted not listening to that small voice inside," I said.

"I call it The Knower," he said. "The Knower knows... if I'm quiet enough inside to hear. I may not like what it says, but it tells the truth. It's located here in my solar plexus." He touched his middle where his stomach was. "And in its brilliant way, if I'm not hearing it, then it starts poking me."

As I listened, I touched the area at the bottom of my ribs where my stomach was.

He continued, "When I don't hear it, that area of my body begins to send messages. It contracts and sometimes hurts, or it gets so tight it feels like I can't breathe deeply enough. My digestion gets off kilter. It says, 'Are you hearing me *now?*' as my body experiences sensations that *do* get my attention." He chuckled. "Rather clever of the body's architect if you ask me."

I was still puzzled. "So, if the 'Knower' is talking and I can't hear it, I just pay attention to an upset stomach?"

"Yes. But you can bypass the indigestion or tight diaphragm by just getting quiet and listening," he answered.

"Then you're saying the key is to quiet my mind so I *can* hear." He nodded. "Do you mean by working on ignoring the past and future thoughts, like we've talked about?"

"An excellent tool to continue working with. But this isn't an either/or scenario. All tools build on each other and there are many. You could also meditate."

I didn't see *that* coming from this eighty-one-year-old man. "I've tried," I told him. "I've used several different methods. I don't get much out of it."

He leaned back and nodded toward the cats. I looked over and they were both sitting on top of the rock cave, watching something in the tree that provided entertainment, as well as shade. They were as still as two figurines. Once again, I was impacted by their ability to be present in the moment, perhaps one of their greatest survival skills.

He turned back to me. "I didn't get much out of it, either. I tried all kinds of ways: guided, unguided, mantras, watching my thoughts, repeating one word silently over and over, prayer, listening to tapes… you name it. Abel offered another simple option."

"I'd like to hear it, especially if it will help me listen to that small voice inside," I said.

"First," Doc said, "find a place to sit, comfortable enough that you won't have to change positions. Don't lie down; you'll just go to sleep." He grinned. "Close your eyes and take a few deep breaths. Then, for fifteen minutes, don't move a muscle. If your nose itches, too bad. Sorry if you want to move your hips, shoulder, or toe. You can't—not even your eyelashes."

I waited for him to finish but he said nothing. "Then what?" I asked.

He smiled. "That's it."

"Well, if that's all there is, when does the spiritual part come in? Or the being present part? Or the hearing the Knower part?" Before he could respond, I added, "And I thought we were working to get the mind quiet, not the body."

He nodded. "It seems backwards, doesn't it? Those who meditate know that as the mind quiets down, the body gets more relaxed and calms down too. The problem for me was that I had to use my mind to go through whatever procedure was needed to *make* that same mind be quiet. One meditation said to watch my thoughts, another said to watch my body, or repeat a word over and over. It didn't make sense to use my mind to create no thoughts. So I did the opposite and quieted the body first. Voila, the mind went quiet also. I don't know how or why, but it works for me."

"What do you mean? What happens? Do you go into a void or fly around the universe? What?" I wasn't trying to be obtuse; I just didn't get the point of it.

"You'll have to discover for yourself what happens when there is stillness of mind and body. I can't describe it well. Let me just say, there is an awareness… a watcher, a beingness that is connected to us. It seems to long for integration into who and what I think I am." He shook his head. "That's all I'll say, or I'll contaminate it with words." He paused again. "Try it if you want to. Just make sure you don't move, which is hard at first. We're not used to being still. If fifteen minutes is too long, try ten, or five." He grinned. "Or not at all. I will add, however, it might be interesting to try it a few times before you toss it for good."

I wasn't sure how far I would get. I fidgeted sometimes. I had adopted the idea that if I was moving, I was doing. If I was doing, I was accomplishing. If I was accomplishing, I was worthwhile. However, at this moment, I saw that as a sad way to determine my own value.

I looked over at the cats, who were now resting on their sides, stretched out with bodies nestled into the cool grass. I thought how good it must be to lie with your nose in the growing green.

Thus began a unique week in my life. I brought Cochon two more times for daytime visits, returning in the evening to take him home. But at Doc's invitation, I came every morning around eight, sipped coffee in his back yard, and listened as he told many stories and answered my many questions. He answered patiently, honestly, and without flourish as he shared what he had learned, both from the man, Abel, and from his eighty-plus years of life experience. He provided examples of how he incorporated what he learned into his relationships, his work, and his understanding of life. It was fascinating. It was uplifting.

And sometimes, it was a little unsettling as I began to observe how much I had blithely accepted as true. Me, the independent thinker, had become dependent on countless people and organizations that I had accepted as my authorities. There was so much I had never questioned.

I brought a notebook and pen and jotted down what I wanted to remember, explore, and think about later. Before I returned the next day, a page of questions would blossom. Most days, I went alone. Though invited, Emma had been busy with late harvest and meetings for the state fair. Then, one morning she was free and came with me. Again, we discussed the past, that deadfall that pulled us away from the present.

She mentioned a call from her sister. "She was so angry the phone handle got hot." She laughed. "I'm not a marriage counselor, but I think she's emasculatin' her husband and it's painful to watch. I don't know what to say to her." Doc asked her if she could give an example.

Emma prefaced her examples by sharing that she thought he was a good man at heart. But he was poor at expressing himself and lacked confidence, so they ended up with a bucketful of misunderstandings. Emma described her sister as having a "Dart List"—a running inventory of his failures. He didn't remember her birthday last year, ignored what she wanted for yesterday's anniversary, didn't take her side when she was criticized by a friend two years ago, drove erratically and scared her six years ago while on vacation, and they didn't get married in the church she wanted. "*That* was twenty-six years ago," she said, a bewildered look on her face.

I winced. "What makes you call it a 'Dart List'?"

"Because," Emma said, "nothin' is ever over. When she gets upset about one thing, she goes down the list and throws her darts. You forgot this, you didn't do that, blah-blah-blah. She brings up everything to prove her point—that he's selfish and doesn't love her enough. She throws every bad memory at him like a dart. Sometimes, I wonder if he's bleedin' inside. I can't conceive how it would feel to always be reminded of my failin's. I've watched my precious sister become bitter, and a decent man become an insecure man. He thinks the only thing he can do is try to not get in her way, do what little he can to please her, and tolerate being her human dartboard."

Emma sighed. "But it's never good enough. He told me once she'd find somethin' wrong if he handed her the Taj Mahal." Her eyes watered a little and she dipped into her pocket for her hanky. "It's so sad that sometimes I cry."

I reached over and squeezed her hand.

"It's more common than you think. People love to pass the buck. It's a great way to avoid taking responsibility. The problem is the dart thrower feels so much anger, hurt, and self-pity that it's harder on them than it is on the one they're blaming." He paused and shook his head. "It's even worse when we blame ourselves. Go ahead, pick on yourself over and over and see how you feel. Repeatedly criticize and blame yourself and eventually it destroys your confidence, peace of mind, and your health... It's dangerous."

"Is there anything I can say or do that will help?" Emma asked, looking at both of us.

"Not until one of them asks," Doc answered.

"That reminds me of what Jake said one time," I told them. "That we can be harmful if we try to give that which hasn't been requested."

Doc nodded. "How true. And until they do ask, that person sees themselves as a victim. Neither is a victim. They both have choices. Asking for assistance is one of them."

"No, she hasn't asked. But I still wonder, why is she doing this? She has two beautiful kids, a great home, money in the bank. She wants for nothing. Why this behavior?" Emma asked in a strained voice.

I thought there were probably many things this woman wanted, but none of them were tangible.

"Maybe there's a better question, Emma. Asking 'why' is typically pointless. It's the mind's way of looking for blame. Assigning blame won't change a thing. Also, asking 'why' sounds punitive—you know 'Why'd you do *that?*' makes the hackles on the back of our necks go up. Instead of asking 'Why is she doing this?' use 'what' instead. Try, 'What's going on that she's so angry?' Does that feel different?"

Emma nodded. "It does... very different. If I ask myself that way, I think she's mad at herself, not him."

"Perceptive," Doc said. "And true. As long as it's your fault, I'm not responsible for my own life." There was dead silence as his words sunk in.

Emma sat back and sighed. "Talkin' about this helps. I like usin' 'what' instead of 'why'. I even feel less anxious when I use 'what'. It feels more... oh... interested in what's goin' on. Not whinin' about what's goin' on." She paused, then asked, "Is there anything else I can pay attention to, Doc?"

"I'll add one thing. If there's no dartboard, there's no place to throw the darts. Perhaps one day Mr. Dartboard will quit playing that role. When he finally tells her it's not acceptable anymore and leaves the room when she throws the first dart, he will give her a great gift."

Emma nodded. "Thank you for that, Doc. You just reminded me of something I forgot."

"What's that" I asked.

"It takes two to tango," she said, grinning. I never forgot that conversation.

∾

The day arrived when I was ready to pick up Cochon from his last visit with MJ. Before I could leave, a truck pulled up. Jake got out and held up a sack. "Yá'át'ééh! Aunt's homemade tortillas—brought you a bunch!" he called.

"Yah-ha-tay! We've missed you, Jake!" We hugged, both tickled to see each other. It had been a few months since we'd visited, and it was a joy to see his kind face. I told him I was getting ready to pick up Cochon and asked if he wanted to come with me. "Of course!" he replied. "I've never even seen Cochon, so I'm looking forward to this. Let me get something first."

I took his sack inside and opened it to find two stacks of flour tortillas, perfectly thick and slightly browned. As Jake ran back to his truck, I wrapped up half of them for Doc.

He returned with a small, flat package in his hand. After I said goodbye to Deidre, she walked over to Jake. He smoothed her head and back. "You are a beautiful one, aren't you?" he murmured to her. And true to her nature, she licked his hand, rubbed her head against his long fingers, then moved her whole body against his legs to let him know he hit the nail on the head.

At Doc's, Jake grabbed his package, and we went to the back yard. Doc was tightening a screw on the Cat Condo as we entered. "Hey, Doc," I called.

He tightened it one last time, then turned around. "Hello there!" he called. And on seeing Jake he said, "Yah-tah-hey, Jake Binally, if my memory serves me." He walked to Jake, extending his hand.

Jake shook it warmly. "Hosteen Parsons, it's an honor to greet you." I handed Doc the tortillas and we hugged. Then, I went to see Cochon and cuddle a moment as MJ sat, eyes moving back and forth as he watched all of us. I got a nudge from the Knower. Doc and Jake had met before, and they both held each other in significant regard.

Doc invited us to sit, and went inside with the tortillas, returning in a minute with three tall glasses. "Sun tea. Hope you like it—lemongrass and hibiscus." We each took a sip. It was a beautiful rose color, and delicious.

Jake handed his package to Doc. "I was going to find out where you lived and drop this off for you today after she and I visited. Now, here we are. I've brought a small gift for you." Inside were two baggies: one of leaves and one with dried, reddish roots.

"Yerba Mansa. How did you know?" Doc asked, grinning broadly.

"I remembered. You came to one of my talks on native plants and wildcrafting a couple years ago. You asked many questions about this plant and its properties. It is a powerful part of the earth's offerings for healing, and I sensed you knew this. This is last year's harvest. In a month or so, this year's harvest should be ready. If you'd like, I'll bring you more. What you have in your hands moves water and clears inflammation, as I'm sure you know. Enjoy it, Hosteen Parsons."

I was intrigued by Jake's use of 'Hosteen', a Navajo term that meant more than 'Mr'. It was also a term of respect and honor.

"Other than your class, have you two met before?" I asked.

"No," Jake said. "But he is honored by the people of Isleta. They tell stories of animals he has saved and hands he has held. You are highly regarded." He smiled at Doc.

"Thank you, Jake," Doc said, nodding his head like a little bow.

Then, we effortlessly talked and listened to each other for over an hour as the sun began its time for slumber. There was no ego vying for attention, no interrupting, just a harmony of words and understanding. Once in a while I would look over at the cats. They were at ease, seeming to relax even more with the quiet conversation. Periodically, MJ would sit and watch us, his copper eyes changing through the many shades of orange and gold as the sun dropped lower.

When it was time to go, Jake turned to Doc. "May I?" was all he said. Doc nodded. He walked quietly to the Condo door and opened it. I shot a look at Doc, expecting him to ask Jake to not enter. He just looked at me with a tiny smile that said it was fine.

Jake closed it quietly and sat on the stump nearest the door. He leaned forward, elbows on his knees, hands relaxed between them. I held my breath as MJ, the cat who avoided humans, walked over to Jake and sat near his feet, looking up at him. Cochon was curled in a ball, asleep by the fountain and its quietly falling water. He didn't stir.

Then, words fell from Jake's mouth like a Female Rain as he spoke his native tongue to MJ in a low, breathy voice, almost a whisper. Silence followed as the two looked at each other. He began chanting, so softly I could barely hear. He sang words I didn't understand in a melody that sounded like wind in the trees mingled with the earth's heartbeat. Still MJ sat, unmoving. When the song ended, he reached inside his shirt and pulled out a medicine bundle attached to a leather cord around his neck. I knew of them but had never seen one; it seemed so small to carry such big medicine. He pinched something inside, then sprinkled it above the big cat. He lifted his hands, palms up, whispered to MJ, and returned to the table.

During the few minutes Jake and MJ spent together, part of me wanted to look away, as if the door to a private conversation had been left open. Doc had leaned back and shut his eyes, but I couldn't. I marveled at MJ's behavior. I felt if I didn't see these things for myself, I would never believe they happened.

I was also touched by Jake's attitude. He had approached MJ with respect, almost a reverence, that was visible in his stature, movements, and voice. As crazy as it seemed to me, Jake app-roached MJ as an equal.

It was time to go, so I went to the Condo and set down the carrier. Cochon had awoken and joined me, meowing. He was ready to go home and walked into it without coaching. I said goodbye to MJ, and he surprised me by walking over and brushing his head against my arm. I touched his face and scratched under his chin lightly. "What a gift you are to all of us. I wish you could know that," I told him. I felt myself starting to tear up, so I added, "And... you're coming home in two days! Hang in there, buddy." Doc and I hugged, then Jake surprised Doc and hugged him also.

Rather than go home and cook, we decided Blake's Lotaburger, a New Mexico institution, would be a perfect ending to the day. On our way there, Jake turned to look at Cochon. "That's quite remark-able, considering what you told me of his former self."

"Carlita from down the street said it was un milagro," I told him.

"A miracle," he said, turning to study Cochon again. Cochon was asleep again in the carrier. I knew he would be fine while we ate. We ordered their famous green chile cheeseburgers. Jake had two of the large double burgers and, not for the first time, I was awed by his appetite.

As we sat outside the little restaurant at a cement table, Jake talked about his experience with MJ. "His eyes tell me he is very old." He paused, choosing his words. "I felt something ancient or timeless. I sang him an honoring song; he is a great warrior."

"What did you sprinkle on him?"

"Corn pollen," he said. "He blessed me. Perhaps that sounds strange. I have received an animal blessing before, but never from a cat. I blessed him in return." Jake slowly chewed his food, his dark eyes looking out at the people, the few cars that passed, the life around him. Night was covering the land like a soft blanket. I pulled my sleeves down as the cooler air joined the darkness.

"May I ask what you whispered to him at the last?"

Jake nodded, swallowing. He took a sip of his drink and crumpled the paper bag and napkins, then lobbed them into a nearby receptacle and turned to me. "Nizhóní," he smiled. "It means beautiful or pretty. Nizhóní permeates the universe. It is the good and true, the harmony and balance that we carry within, as well as that which exists without. It is the bedrock of Ho'zho'... walking in beauty in the world." He paused and we were quiet as that world moved around us.

"MJ is nizhóní," I said, then paused to see if I could find the right words. Jake waited, ever the consummate listener. "He brings the qualities with him he seems to instill in others: patience, kindness, confidence, timelessness. He's been seminal in a transformation which there is no word for except miraculous. And because of the gifts he has given to Cochon, I have changed too. At times, I feel like I'm on an accelerated course toward something that is huge and bright and terrible. Terrible in a beautiful way." Saying that moved me in a deep place inside. But it was a feeling I couldn't describe.

Jake laid his big hand over mine and pressed it gently, nodding. Saying nothing.

"I doubt if that makes any sense," I said, suddenly feeling weary.

"Most of life does not make sense," he said softly. "I am not sure it is supposed to. Where is the sweetness if we have to distill such an experience down into what can be measured, proven, or rendered semantically perfect?"

We drove home, and before parting, we hugged. Once again, he kissed the top of my head and whispered, "Go in beauty, my friend." And once again, it felt like a blessing.

He got in his truck and started to leave, then backed up and stopped, rolling down the window. I had just let Cochon inside and turned to look at him. "Forget something?" I smiled and walked over.

"One more thing," he said, quietly. "Putting something holy into words never makes sense, except to the one who experiences it." He drove away.

20

A Male Rain

"We have not merely escaped from something,
but also into something...
We have joined the greatest of all communities,
which is not that of man alone,
but of everything which shares with us the great adventure
of being alive."
– Joseph Wood Krutch

MJ came back in style, riding in the front seat in a kennel lined with sheepskin. Doc played a tape of Vivaldi's 'Four Seasons' for him— his welcome home song. Doc wanted him to "hear the good parts," so he drove the long, roundabout way to my house through the countryside. Near the Mackland farm, he stopped and lifted the kennel out so MJ could see their horses running in the field. He said MJ was attentive and seemed impressed.

They arrived close to nine in the morning that first week of September. About ten minutes before they drove up, Cochon hopped onto the deep windowsill by the front door. Though MJ had been away for two weeks, their connection remained strong.

I was drying dishes when Cochon meowed in his now rather loud voice. I let him outside, just as Doc's Travelall pulled in. Deidre hopped onto the warm spot he'd left behind and watched from the windowsill.

Doc was already opening the passenger door to retrieve his precious cargo. I waited on the deck with Cochon as he brought the carrier and set it down. MJ yowled and began to move about. "Ready?" Doc asked me. I must have been grinning like a fool because he laughed and opened the door. MJ almost bounded out, then stopped. He yowled again, perhaps his own "welcome home to me" moment.

Cochon pranced over and nudged him. MJ made a throaty, purring-like sound and licked the top of his head. Doc sat down and patted the chair beside him. We both were still, not talking, watching as MJ satisfied his own need to reorient himself. He walked around the deck, sniffing everything: boards, furniture, potted plants, a stray leaf. I studied him and thought his hair had grown quite a bit in two weeks, but he still had pale swaths of skin showing through that made him look dappled.

Unable to stay still, Cochon suddenly sprinted toward the back of the house. MJ watched, then walked away, following him. "Is he okay?" I asked Doc, unused to seeing him so uninspired and slow.

He nodded. "Just getting his sea legs. He hasn't done that kind of running in a couple weeks. I get a feeling he's doing some internal checking. It may take him a day or two to return to his usual agility," he said without a speck of concern in his voice. I wasn't as sure.

But we didn't have to wait two days. From around the opposite side of the house ran Cochon, MJ running at top speed behind him. Inside myself, I jumped up and cheered a thousand yesses.

Doc and I watched as they tumbled in the soft grass before MJ took off with Cochon behind him. They ran, leapt high in the air, twisted, and chased each other—first, one up the bur oak, then the other one up the cottonwood by the barn. Deidre joined us and sat in my lap as we watched, mesmerized by the explosive energy of their joy. Doc and I caught ourselves spontaneously laughing and clapping as the Water Brothers gave the performance of a lifetime.

In a few minutes, Emma and Gus walked over. Gus was carrying a rather large wood contraption. It looked like he was struggling a bit and Doc jumped up. "Can I help, Gus?"

"No, I got 'er," he said, puffing a little. Emma reached down and lifted a part of it the last few steps. Everyone hugged and Gus turned toward the cats. "Got 'im all stitched up, I see. Durn if he doesn't look worse 'n ever." He chuckled, then he turned to me, saying kindly, "But we're mighty glad he's home and your little 'un has his friend back." He looked out at Cochon. "Not so little anymore, seems like." He studied him a moment. Then, he told us there were a couple more items to bring over and left.

"He's been so excited to finish this project, he can barely contain himself," Emma said. "That man has the best ideas, I swear." Doc followed him over to see if he needed any help. Emma watched as the cats ran again toward the back. "He looks real good, doesn't he?" she said. "He acts like the only thing that happened was he got a bad haircut." Both of us grinned. I could tell we were both feeling the same thing—a final release of concern for the cat who brought so much and asked so little.

Gus and Doc walked back, another wooden piece and various tools in their hands. I offered to cook breakfast, but everyone had eaten except me, so Emma and I went inside. "Mmm, mmm... somethin' smells good," she said, sniffing the air. I told her I put a roast in the oven, a celebration meal for MJ's homecoming. I didn't cook beef often and it was a treat for all of us. Even Deidre and Cochon enjoyed chopped roast with juice.

An hour later, Gus called us to join them outside. He pointed to the front of the house to my left. There stood a beautifully crafted wooden box on a sturdy base. Gus took my arm and did the honors. "The openin' is thirty-two inches off the ground, low enough for that ol' coot to jump up right easy. An' high enough to keep them coyotes and coons out." Over the opening he had glued two letters he had painstakingly carved in beautiful script: "MJ".

"Go on. Reach inside and feel." He stepped back so I could get closer. The interior was soft but made a crunching sound when I pressed it. "It's good natural straw. Emma made a thick flannel cover." He pulled it out through the hole, showing me what looked like a bumpy pillow. "She even put one of them zippers on it so you can restuff it, like that scarecrow o' Dorothy's." He chuckled at the thought. "Now feel the walls inside." I ran my hand across something corrugated and slick. "It's insulation fer top, bottom, and sides—some new contraption I found that don't have any o' them fibers in it. Jes nice n' smooth. Kinda looks like aluminum (he pronounced it al-you-minium). I cut it with a boxcutter. Can you imagine that?" Doc had to peek inside to see what it was too, possibly considering how he could use it in the Cat Condo.

I was overcome with gratefulness and Gus hugged me, then winked. "I don't know why, but you and that grey un' took a shine to ol' ugly. So, Emma and I wanted 'im to be warm come winter. Also made 'im a door flap outa rubber—it'll keep them winds outta it. I'll attach it in November thereabout." He grinned like the Cheshire Cat. He had on overalls. If they'd had buttons, they would have popped he was so proud.

"You don't know what a relief this is to me to know he has a place to go when winter comes. Thank you so much. It's just beautiful," I told them, and Doc and Emma chimed in to brag on his work of art. I told them I was going to call it the "Studio" since it was complete in one room. I crossed my fingers mentally, hoping he would use it.

That evening, I fed MJ half of his bowl of roast at the base of his new sleeping quarters. Then, I put more inside the Studio. His nose found it and he easily jumped into the opening. He ate, then jumped out again. I could hear Doc's voice in my mind saying it would take time. I sat a while on the deck, watching them explore, always aware of their surroundings and each other. I looked out at the trees that were changing, and I fell in love with the Bosque all over again.

People said that particular fall was one of the most beautiful they had ever seen. The cottonwoods turned a radiant yellow, as they did each year when the cooler days and nights arrived. Near the river, willow and salt cedar pulled their energy back down into their roots. Trees wore every shade of yellow, orange, and gold imaginable. But to see the startling red of maple trees that decorated the Midwest each fall, I had to drive to Fourth of July Canyon in the Manzano Mountains. There, the Bigtooth maples erupted in blazing red. Couched next to the perfect yellow of the scrub oaks, the green pines, and the blue sky, I thought the canyon was well named. The whole drive was like a celebration. Apples were in season, and on the way home I bought a dozen from one of the roadside stands. They were fire engine red and so juicy you needed a napkin.

In mid-September, Emma won second place in the state fair pie contest. She was thrilled, telling me her blueberry peach pie was the best she'd ever made. She said second place was just fine. The word 'place' was the one that really mattered.

Doc, Jake, and I gathered for a cookout at Gus and Emma's. The next month, we did the same at Doc's. We all contributed food, laughter, and a flowing conversation that moved like dancing water over time-worn stones. Our words became a kind of music that sang an honoring song of mysteries and friendship, change and love. It sang of beauty.

The neighborhood had its ritual fall potluck on a bright day in October. Our small group was joined by Carlita and her husband, Miguel, who had surprised her for their second-year anniversary and gotten leave from the Army. Her tummy had made up for lost time and she looked like she had a volleyball under her blouse. She and her husband were healthy, glowing, and attentive to each other in such a way it squeezed your heart to see it. The whole Sanchez family came, including Manny and Coco, who Manny always called Mamacita, and the three little ones who ran and giggled and screamed exuberantly. Five other families joined us from our street, complete with enough children to have a good game of dodgeball, with Gus as referee.

We also invited Sissy and Barry Mackland and, of course, Ferrari. The Sanchez children fell in love with the burly dog. He Who Ran Like The Wind acted like he could barely tolerate all this hugging and fawning nonsense. Barry said it was all show; he loved it. Carol the Egg Lady and her husband, Dave, joined us too. Emma said she invited them and the Macklands because they lived in the midst of farmland, with no close-by neighbors. So, at the cookout, by unanimous consent, all five—including Ferrari—were made honorary neighbors.

Emma and I both went to the Balloon Fiesta in October, just in time to see the evening ascension and hear her new favorite "young folks" band, Three Dog Night. I had never seen Emma dance and she moved inside the music. We cheered and clapped and swayed with each other, with strangers, and all by ourselves. For one evening, the lines in her face simply disappeared.

The rains didn't affect any of the festivities, and when they did come that fall, they were hard Male Rains that moved quickly on to leave clear skies and the rich smells of the land in transition. The chamisa and grasses turned golden brown. Jake wildcrafted by the river, thanking the Yerba Mansa for its life as he gathered it from the muddy, sandy soil beneath the cottonwoods. All was in balance. All was good.

After Balloon Fiesta, I began making my lists for the Fourth Annual Widows and Orphans Dinner—shopping list, menu list, supply list, grocery list, call list to spread the word again, and the call list of prior attendees. Doc, Jake, Emma, and Gus were also spreading the word.

Doc offered extra folding chairs, tables, and linens, Gus would rake leaves to tidy the yard, and Emma would make pies. Jake said he would bring a big pot of Three Sisters Soup with mutton. Depending on how many we could squeeze in, my four friends hoped to attend. Doc agreed. At certain times in our lives, all of us had been widows and orphans.

The cats loved the fall too. Sometimes Deidre and Cochon didn't come in until they were called at bedtime. The weather was too comfortable, there were too many bugs to chase, too many sweet spots to nap in, and too many skittering leaves that taunted them to catch-me-if-you-can. Their fall world was ripe with new smells and sounds to explore and remember. MJ's hair grew back, and he acted as if he never been manhandled by an overzealous Great Horned Owl.

MJ stayed out of the new Studio for over a week. Then, one night, I peered through the window and saw a long black foot dangling out. That night, I slept deeper than I had in a long time. Finally, he had a safe place in the dark.

Every day began the same: MJ waiting on the deck for breakfast and Deidre and Cochon waiting inside. MJ didn't miss meals very often. If Cochon was inside, he would still go off by himself to run the ditch banks and explore his world. But he usually managed to be back at our door by breakfast or dinner, and many times he was there for both. He began sleeping in his Studio most nights. He never came in the greenhouse again.

He and Cochon seemed to grow even closer, spending more and more time together. The first time they didn't come home, I had a strong worry knot in my stomach and began to think of all the ways they could be hurt.

I mentioned it to the group when we had the cookout at Gus and Emma's. "Back they come... all those thoughts of fear. Thoughts of anger at myself for letting Cochon roam after dinner. I wish I could reach a point where I didn't go into full tilt worry. I wish I could banish those kinds of thoughts forever. What do you do?" I asked, looking at all of them.

Doc was in Emma's kitchen getting the pitcher of tea, and called out, "Don't believe everything you think!" He chuckled and we joined him.

Emma looked at us and said, "I just think of it as traffic on the street, honey. Never once in my life did I run out to stop a car to see what it was like." She smiled.

Doc joined us and refilled our teas. "Good one, Emma." Then he turned to me. "It takes time and lots of practice. Changing a habit or perspective isn't a drive-thru where you get your result in a couple minutes. Be patient."

Jake cleared his throat, then said quietly, "What I push, pushes back. I don't try to get rid of the dark thoughts or get involved with them. They aren't me, so I just watch them pass by like people walking past on a busy street. They disappear. Usually fairly quickly." We all nodded. Then we turned to Gus.

Gus was looking at the floor. He shifted his body, looked up, and said, "I'm not a very complicated man, so I jes' see it in a simple way: These here thoughts y'all are talkin' about make feelins, what Emma calls 'moods.' So I reckon since I'm gonna walk around in some kinda mood all day anyway, it might as well be one I enjoy." He nodded his head firmly, his way of letting us know there was nothing else to say. He was a man of few words, but the words he and the others shared were pure gold.

⟋⟍⟋

In the third week of October, I was watching the news and heard thunder rumbling in the distance. I walked outside and called Cochon and MJ, but there was no answer except a bird call coming from the barn. I looked at the sky and couldn't see any stars. I stepped away from the house and saw lightning in the northwest sky. I went back in, hoping the cats got home before the rain started. A couple minutes later, a thunderclap made Deidre and I jump, then lightning brightened the landscape.

A Male Rain had come and the skies opened up in a torrent of water. It poured so hard it sounded like drums on the roof. I stood at the door under the overhang, watching for the cats. Then the thunder clapped, immediately followed by lightning, and I went inside and sat back down to watch a special weather report. It warned of flooding near the river. I said to myself, "I am afraid right now for the cats." I didn't try to not be afraid or beat myself up for feeling that way. I didn't try to change the feeling or push it away, and within seconds, the fear receded and I relaxed.

It was in that relaxed state that I heard the Knower, not in words but through an urging compulsion. "Get up. Open the door." I immediately did and looked out into a sheet of water. I saw nothing as thunder clapped overhead, and when lightning followed like a floodlight, I saw a blur on the street running at breakneck speed.

Cochon bolted down the drive, into the yard, and through the front door. He was going so fast that he skidded on the tile floor and thumped into a kitchen cupboard. Then he ran down the hallway and disappeared as I stood at the door, thinking MJ was behind him. When he didn't immediately come running too, I ran to check on Cochon.

I grabbed several towels and looked for him in the bedroom, then the office. No Cochon. I looked under the bed and under the desk. Finally, I opened all the closet doors until I found him in the bedroom, a wet wad of dark fur shaking so hard he looked like he was having convulsions. I draped a towel over him, lifted him up and sat on the bed, rubbing him vigorously. Still he shook. I grabbed another dry towel and continued rubbing, cooing, and talking quietly, calmly. Deidre hopped onto the bed as I sat there, trying to dry his shaking body.

She licked his paw and nudged him as I dried, whispering over and over, "It's alright, sweet boy. Everything is fine. Shh-shh-shh..." As he became drier, his shaking began to calm, and I checked him all over for injuries but found none. All I could figure out was he had been terrified by the storm and was separated from MJ. But really, I hadn't figured out anything. I just wanted him to feel dry and warm and loved.

I offered him food, but he ignored it. I carried him to the living room and sat on the couch, still drying parts of his long fur. Deidre sat very close, purring. When he struggled to leave, I let him. When we went to bed, he was already asleep under the covers. During the night, I got up a couple times and stepped onto the deck to look in MJ's Studio, but it stayed empty.

I awoke before dawn and Cochon was already gone. Deidre meowed her "good morning, and isn't breakfast a good idea?" meow. I started the coffee, then prepared their bowls, and set out MJ's bowl full of leftover chicken from last night.

"Cochon!" I called. But he didn't come. After looking in all the usual spots, I found him in the bedroom closet again, tucked in the back, curled into a tight ball on top of a sweater that had slipped off its hanger. I crawled in under the hanging clothes and smoothed his head and back. He meowed softly and licked my finger, then went back to sleep.

I washed up and got dressed, then stepped outside to check the Studio. I was so sure MJ would be passed out too. But it was empty. It was after six. It bothered me a little, but I knew he'd head back when he got hungry enough.

I put down food for Deidre, got a mug of coffee, put on a heavy sweater, and went back outside to watch the beginning of sunrise on a glorious day. The rain had washed off the residue of dust from the winds before the storm. The grass and trees sparkled. As I watched the light slowly intensify, I hummed "Beauty All Around," the song that spoke of the balance and harmony of all things, and I slowly relaxed into my body. It was a moment of pure peace, like when I was seven with my boulders on Sugar Creek, completely safe and at ease. I started to doze...

I awoke when I heard footsteps on the gravel. I looked up, surprised I had dozed off, but happy to see Emma and Gus walking over. "Good morning!" I called. "You're early birds, the sun hasn't broken the crest yet." I walked over to give them a hug.

"Got some coffee, honey?" Emma asked. I looked at her face and knew something was wrong.

"What is it? What's wrong?" I asked. Emma just smiled and shook her head.

Gus sat down in a chair. "I sure could use a cup of coffee, little girl." I got two steaming mugs and brought them out, setting them down on the little table between them.

I watched them closely. "Something's happened. What is it?"

Emma reached out and took my hand and looked into my eyes. "Honey, Gus went out early this mornin' to drive around. He wanted to see if there were any branches that might be in the roads after that big ol' storm last night."

He interrupted her, "Yup, bound to be a branch or two I could haul off to the side. Got stopped jes around the corner on the loop road. Car went into a ditch last night and Darryl from the gas station was hookin' it up to tow. He waved and I asked him if the driver was okay and he said the guy, plain and simple, couldn't see 'cause a the rain bein' so heavy. He jes plum drove off in the ditch." He stopped, took a sip of his coffee, then cleared his throat.

"Well, while I was a'helpin' Daryl hook up the car, I saw somethin' in the grass and..." He paused again. "It were MJ."

Emma squeezed my hand and looked carefully at me. "Honey, he's dead. He must'a been hidin' in the grass on the side and when that car went off the road, it hit him. Gus said he was killed instantly."

I stared at them both, feeling cold inside. "I want to see him. You brought him home, didn't you? I want to see him." I could hear my voice taking on a tone that said I don't believe you... I don't believe you at all.

Gus shook his head. "You don't want to see him, missie. He's a mess. That car plum run over 'im." He paused. "I'm gonna make 'im a nice wooden box to be buried in. It'll be right fine."

I'm not sure I can describe what happened in that moment, but I felt nothing except an imperative to identify his body. I wouldn't believe he was dead unless one of the three who knew him best—Cochon, Doc, or me—had checked this cat out thoroughly and affirmed it was MJ. I felt no sadness, no loss, not even a sense of shock. I was all business, buoyed by the need for affirmation and decisiveness.

I looked at Gus and said quietly, "No. There's nothing fine about any of this. I want to see his body. Maybe it's another black cat that looks like him and you're mistaken."

Emma squeezed my hand again, which she hadn't let go of. "Honey, that right ear was all chewed up, that thin strip was missing down his front right leg, the little crescent moon patch of missing hair on his cheek, the bent tail... it was MJ."

You can't say this. You saw what you wanted to see because the cat was black and big.

I let go of her hand and leaned back. "Thank you for finding that cat, Gus. I'll be over later to identify it *if* it's MJ. Right now, I need to check on Cochon. He ran home in the middle of the storm, and he's upset and back to hiding in closets. Please excuse me. I need time, I need space," I heard myself say in my most polite and quiet voice. And then something shifted as my awareness of what they were saying caused the tiniest crack in my hard crust of denial. A stranger's voice came out of my mouth as it said, "What I *need* is for this to not happen. What I *need* is for him to be alive." I went back inside and shut the door.

I began washing dishes. I thought about nothing. Me, who was so aware of the thoughts that vied for attention in my mind, had none. I wasn't upset, angry, or sad. I was nothing. I went to the closet and Cochon was sound asleep, curled in a tight ball, his fluffy tail covering his eyes. One thought arose: *Do cats cry?*

I wrote checks for bills, put stamps on envelopes, swept the kitchen floor, and I was aware of a knocking sound—*Is Gus building something in his garage?*—but I ignored it. Then, the knock became louder, and I heard Doc's voice, "Are you home?" It was my own door and I opened it. I didn't invite him in. "Hi," he said. "I cleaned up the cat, and you can come over, if you have a minute, and identify the body." He said this comfortably, as if he were offering me to take a look at a new book he'd purchased. I didn't say anything, just followed him over to Gus and Emma's garage.

On Gus's worktable was a small pallet. On top was a cat who laid on its side, covered from the shoulders down with a small, blue blanket, the size which a newborn might be wrapped in. Emma and Gus weren't there, and Doc walked away.

I went to the cat and stared at it for a long time. Finally, I reached out and touched its head. *He has the most noble head.* Immovable. Not even the skin moved over its skull. *Death makes us stiff.* The eyes were open, and I got down very close to its face and looked at them. They were dark, flat. But when I slowly searched their surface, I could see minute specks of copper. *Why would you take the light from his eyes?* I slowly moved my hand down the cat's body and it was all wrong—concaved or bony or bulging in spots that didn't belong there.

"Who are you?" I whispered and my hand reached out to smooth its brow, the side of its cheek. I lifted the stiff head and looked at the right ear. I'd always thought MJ's ragged ear looked like the edge of one of my mom's doilies. There it was. *It was the first thing I noticed about you that Thanksgiving morning.* Then I uncovered his tail. It was bent. *What else do I need to see?*

I put my forearms on either side of his body, leaned close to him, and whispered, "MJ, I am so sorry this has happened. Oh God, I am so sorry." I began to cry. I put my forehead against his and let my warm tears flow onto his fur. "Oh, my sweet, beautiful, ancient, and wise boy. Oh God, how I hate this. I hate it!" And suddenly I felt rage like I never had before. It took my breath away and I felt like screaming. "Why? Why! Answer me that, you ridiculous power that squanders the best of this world!" And my heart felt like it was in a vice. The anger stopped as suddenly as it had begun. As my breaths slowed and became less ragged, I whispered, "How terribly and completely you'll be missed." I heard myself crying through the words, crying through my body, crying through the ages as everything stopped to give us time to stretch toward each other and touch each other's hearts one last time.

I cried and cried. I smoothed his broken body and whispered my love and gratitude. I cried for the incalculable loss of his presence in our lives. I cried as I asked him to watch over Cochon. I stroked him from his beautiful head to his broken tail and told him I hoped wherever he was that they appreciated him one tenth as much as we did, and if they didn't to let me know and I'd kick their asses. That made me laugh. And then it made me cry again. I cried until my heart was dry. I cried until there was nothing left.

And then I pulled over a plastic outdoor chair, set it next to the worktable, and leaned my upper body on the pallet with my nose in the fur at the top of his head. I breathed in the last of his scent. I breathed in whatever leftover particles still danced around him that were part of his great spirit. I breathed him in and took him with me forever.

21

Friendship, Pure and Simple

*"The bond that links your true family is not one of blood,
but of respect and joy in each other's life.
Rarely do members of one family grow up under the same roof."
– Richard Bach*

I took a shovel from Gus and Emma's garage and walked to my back yard. There was a fence between my property and the neighbor's field. It was a huge field that stretched so far the trees on the other side looked like miniatures in a diorama. I chose a spot under the large oak that straddled our properties. The tree would provide shade in the summer, brilliant-colored leaves in the fall, and deep roots that would eventually intertwine with MJ's body to make him a part of the land he loved, and it a part of him. I began to dig. After a few minutes, Gus and Doc joined me, shovels in hand.

No one talked as we lifted the rich earth to the side in small mounds. The cats joined us. Cochon climbed the oak, perhaps to get a better look. When we were done, Gus took my shovel and went home with Doc. They returned with a small wooden box in Gus's arms, while MJ laid in Doc's. I asked him to set MJ on the ground so the cats could use their eyes, noses, and ears to learn the story. Deidre walked up immediately and sniffed MJ's head, then down the blue blanket and back up the other side as she walked around him. Then she walked away, content with the story she read. Cochon climbed down from the oak tree and sat, apart and watching.

Just then, Emma came around the back of the house. "Come on, y'all, let's have some breakfast and coffee and let the cats have more time if they want." We joined her inside for warm chorizo, egg, and cheese burritos. She set the table for five, a detail I barely noticed until we heard a truck pull in. "'Bout time." She smiled and went to the door, opening it.

I didn't know she had called Jake, and I was relieved to see his tall, slim form enter the room. He had a leather satchel over his shoulder and almost ceremoniously lifted the strap over his head and set it down. He studied my face for a moment and saw it begin to crumple. In two long steps, he enfolded me in his arms. Tears again. Would I never stop? Jake was a light hugger, but this time he held me tightly as he leaned down to whisper so only I could hear. "My heart, too, is sad. Our tears honor him." He kissed the top of my head.

I sat facing the back door in the kitchen with its full glass storm door. I could see the cats by the little blue blanket and tiny casket. As we all began to eat, I took a bite, but tasted nothing. I excused myself and stood at the door, watching them as they sniffed the growing things, as they crouched and chittered when a bird moved nearby, as they batted bugs and did what they did so well: be themselves. Deidre sat on top of the box for a while and groomed herself, then jumped off. Both of them stood near MJ every so often. Then, Deidre came to the back door, and I let her in. Cochon sat by MJ's body for several minutes more, unmoving. Eventually he joined us too.

The sun had opened itself onto another beautiful fall day. After dishes were washed and dried, we went back to the fence line.

Before he was laid in the box, we took turns sharing a memory. Emma said she would never forget how Cochon kept growing and growing after meeting his Water Brother. "MJ was magic, and we don't get to see enough of that in this old life," she said. Gus told us he would always remember how much he grew to admire him. "He weren't no regular cat. I don't know why, but he made me wanna be kinder," he said. Doc just shook his head and said to us, "He came to teach us through his demonstration. I'll write it down and share what he taught me when I've made sense of it." Then he turned to MJ's body. "You loved us all, without judgment or need. My eternal thanks to you." He wiped a wet spot from under one eye.

Instead of Jake talking, he reached inside the satchel he'd brought and pulled out a feather. It was long with alternating horizontal strips of cream and dark grey—a Great Horned Owl's wing feather, that marvel of creation frayed at the tip to avoid wind turbulence, making its flight almost silent. He placed it on top of MJ, humming and chanting in a quiet, low tone as he sprinkled something from his medicine bundle. Then, he raised his arms, palms up, and whispered, "Go in beauty, my friend."

Gus and Jake began shoveling the rich, black dirt back where it belonged and Doc finished the last of it, tamping the earth down hard with the back of the shovel.

Deidre and Cochon had joined us and watched everything. When it was finished and we headed back to the house, Deidre came with us, but Cochon stayed. He sat down on the newly tamped dirt and watched birds above him in the elm. And we all began life without MJ the warrior, MJ the healer, MJ the teacher whose message was love.

Everyone left, and I sat on the deck, doing nothing, thinking nothing, feeling as if my life was a bowl that had been emptied. I didn't know this land of grief and didn't know how to walk it. Was emptiness normal? I remembered Doc saying once that in medical school he studied what the instructors called "the norm." When he went into practice, he said, "I never did meet Norm." He said no two of us are alike, so we can't be lumped together. There are no standards for people, just for spark plugs. We are unique. I imagined grief was unique too, so I let myself be empty.

Over the next week, Cochon seemed almost fine. He ate well, cuddled and played with Deidre. But other times he wandered almost aimlessly, through the yard, to the mailbox, over the ditch banks into parts unknown. He had short bursts of exuberance that were truncated, perhaps by his own sense of displacement. Some nights, he slept outside in MJ's Studio.

At my request, Doc made a house call, and I put Cochon on the kitchen table so they could sit eye-to-eye. He listened to his heart and checked his body.

"Anything?" I asked after he had gone over him thoroughly.

He took off his stethoscope and shook his head. "Nothing. But sometimes what we can't see is hardest on us." He studied him and listened to my descriptions. "Grief does strange things to animals. I have seen them die shortly after losing their human or a close companion. I've seen them go into depression, quit eating, become angry or so pathetic they can barely find the energy to care for themselves.

"But most animals deal with death in a natural way. They usually handle it better than humans, because they feel no guilt or regret... only loss. Let's just watch and give him time to heal. I'll come back and check on him in a couple weeks." But he never did.

That night, the phone woke me out of a deep sleep. It was my sister who told me Mom had had a stroke that afternoon. The hospital was running more tests, so she didn't have much detail, but she had been at the hospital for hours, scared and overwhelmed. She told me in a tired voice the doctors hoped she would recover most of her right-side body weakness. She couldn't sign her name, but there was no droopy eye or mouth. They weren't as sure about her mental acuity. "She doesn't look good, Sis." Then, in a plaintive voice, she asked, "Can you come home?" I reached out to stroke Cochon and Deidre who were cuddled under the blankets.

"To visit? Or to stay?" I asked. She hesitated, then said at least to visit. She apologized for waking me, but it felt urgent to her. My whole being was on high alert as my sense of foreboding returned, silent since I'd had that strange dream about not hearing my sister's voice.

But I heard her now, and I knew this wouldn't be a visit. If I didn't move back home, I would lose countless opportunities for conversations and experiences and a closure I wouldn't otherwise have. It was a potential loss I couldn't afford. A dispassionate awareness told me Mom wouldn't be around a lot longer. There was no thought or feeling as the kaleidoscope turned the tiniest, almost imperceptible notch and...

Click.

My life changed its course in the space of a heartbeat.

There was no feeling after we hung up, no worry, no fear of what if, no guilt for not going home to visit more often. There was only movement. I removed flattened boxes from a closet, reassembled and taped them and began to pack. *What are you thinking? This is your life, your people, your joy! Go visit—you don't have to leave! What's* wrong *with you?* I ignored the voice that wanted to undermine my decision.

As I wrapped pieces of pottery in newspaper, I thought of my friends. They were my family too, and they understood me in a way no one ever had. They loved me, checked on me, and nurtured me. They poked me when I needed it, but always with love. And when I didn't need it, they wrapped me up in their interest, conversation, and kind deeds.

But there was also a gossamer thread that joined me to my mother; the woman who gave me life, who loved me without question and raised me to be a kind and independent woman. As I had listened to my sister, no matter what she said Mom's prognosis was, I knew without question our mother would leave us. Maybe not in a few weeks or months, but sooner than expected. *It's just a stroke. Lots of people have strokes and go on to live perfectly normal lives!* But underneath the mental chatter, I knew something was *wrong* and it sat like a stone deep in my belly.

At midnight, I finally crawled back into bed.

I awoke before sunrise and donned a heavy robe and slippers as I walked outside in the dark to sip coffee and greet the day. The moon was full, illuminating the bigger structures—the yard and barn, the tops of trees—while shadows hid the details in obscurity. I thought of MJ. He had done better than the moon. He illuminated the bigger things in life as well as the smaller details. I sorely missed his presence.

I whispered to him and told him I was leaving. I asked if he could let me know he was okay. "Can you give me a sign?" I pleaded. "Just something to let me know you are still alive... someplace?"

Maybe I wasn't different than others who decisively say life doesn't end when we die, but secretly wonder what *really* happens. I imagined our essence went on in some form to continue growing and becoming. I had no illusions about angels, harp music, or streets of gold. I didn't know what it would be like, but my hope was I would walk through the veil that separated the living from those who had left. I *wanted* to believe death didn't end me. I didn't want to disappear.

"I just want to know your great spirit still lives, MJ. I don't want you to disappear either," I whispered.

He had brought so many miraculous and magical experiences to our lives since we first met, almost a year ago. Was it too much to ask for one more small piece of magic, one more miracle? His life had been so full of strange wonderment that I half expected his head to pop up in the tall grass by the barn where he used to wait, his notched right ear his calling card. I strained my eyes but saw nothing. I squinted, thinking I might catch a glimpse of his form if I looked in just the exact right way. The grass remained undisturbed.

I scanned the rest of the yard and looked up in the trees in case he was sitting on a branch, but no limb bore his weight. Then, I jumped up as I realized I hadn't checked his Studio. I felt inside and it was empty. The only thing that gave me the slightest tinge of hope was that the straw bed, lovingly covered by Emma in flannel, was slightly warm. I left my hand inside and rested my head against the opening as a few tears watered the deck. I missed him deeply and my heart hurt.

As the sun colored the sky a faint orange above the mountains, I went back inside to shower, dress, and feed the cats. They ate quickly and went out to the deck to explore another dazzling morning in the Bosque. I continued to hope MJ would give me a sign before I moved away. *Are you there?* Something. Anything.

As I was pouring my second cup of coffee, I heard a noise from the back yard that sounded like a low, quiet, choppy hum. I opened the wooden door to peer through the storm door and gasped.

As far as the eye could see, the neighbor's huge alfalfa field was solid white, as if it had snowed a foot overnight. It undulated like a living thing, and the humming sound I heard clearly now was the low "talking" of thousands of pure white snow geese. I quietly stepped outside to behold one of nature's wonders.

These glorious geese had migrated from as far as 1500 miles away in Northern Canada to winter in the Bosque Del Apache, an area south of me that welcomed over three hundred types of birds to its 57,000 acres of forest and wetlands. They were beautiful geese, pure white except for a swath of black on the underside of their wings at the tips. They mated for life and returned yearly. Every morning at sunrise, they joined thousands of Sandhill Cranes as they took off en masse to their chosen grain field for feeding. And each sunset they returned, honking a wild cacophony to announce their arrival.

The sun broke over the mountains, and the whole field gleamed and sparkled like bright sunlight on fresh snow. They took my breath away—the sheer number, the pristine white, the ever-moving, rippling of the bodies as they fed and walked and talked. They moved like a single organism.

I sat on the back stoop and watched for a long time. Then, something I couldn't see or hear startled maybe fifty birds that rose as one and lifted into the sky. Without hesitation another section of the field became airborne, then another bunch, and another, and another, repeated over and over, up and up, until all of them, thousands of them, moved in unison, swirling in a perfectly circular choreographed pattern above me. Around and around, they lifted higher and higher into the blue morning, creating a breath-taking vortex. As I looked up, everywhere was white, swirling movement. I was at the center of a living snow globe.

In some magical way, each bird was connected to all the others as they moved in concert, following a signal only they understood. Was I also connected to them? Perhaps I was, but I felt connected to my own flock: Doc, Gus, Emma, and Jake. And I was leaving the flock.

Could only one bird migrate? Or only one human? Or would we be lost without the rest of the flock? A stark sense of aloneness enfolded me. I didn't want to feel that right now, and I didn't have to yet. I yearned for my friends.

I walked over to see Emma and Gus. They were stunned, both talking at once, careful to say how sorry they were about my mother and agreeing that being with her and my family was a good thing to do. I could also tell that both were sad. I was beyond sad. I would miss them terribly. Before I left, Emma stood up and hugged me fiercely. "I waited sixty years to find a good friend. I'm so glad that it's you." All of our eyes were wet.

Later, I went to Doc's and found him in the back preparing the Cat Condo for possible winter visitors. When I told him, he looked at me with sad eyes and said he would miss me. "You've been a gift to all of us. Without your kindness to a stray cat, none of us would have had these marvelous experiences or learned what we've learned. You are quite special. Don't forget." I watched my shoes in the grass and felt the heat of embarrassment warm my face. He echoed what I said about him and Jake, Gus and Emma. They were a gift to *me. They* were the special ones.

He saw my discomfort and changed the subject, asking how Cochon was doing. I told him about the same: seemingly fine, but still acting "introspective," if I could even give that trait to an animal.

He told me we were woefully ignorant about what animals think or feel. "Just keep an eye on him. And call anytime, okay?" I told him I would. "And by the way, pass your lists for Thanksgiving to all of us and we'll take over for you." I hugged him, suddenly wanting to stop, unpack, quit this crazy idea, and tell him to forget I'd ever mentioned it. "We'll get together and have a real sending off party," he said and hugged me good and hard. As he walked me to my car, he added, "It is your time to leave and share what you've been given. When asked. Only when asked." He squeezed my shoulder and returned to his Cat Condo project.

Jake was harder to reach, but I left a message with his grand-mother for him to call me. When he finally did, he took a deep breath and told me he would miss us. He said I was the kindest, wisest bilagaana he had ever known. "But don't let that go to your head," he chuckled. He also said he would see me soon.

Last, I called my sister. She was thrilled and said my brother would also come so he could drive the U-Haul. She made arrange-ments that day to fly out and help me pack and drive back with the cats. Mom seemed a little better and there were high hopes she would regain her speaking and writing skills with therapy and time. But she still couldn't remember which month it was.

The night before my sister arrived, we had a party at Gus and Emma's for the five of us. After dinner, we put on jackets and sweaters and sat in their back yard near the fire pit Gus had built years ago. We roasted marshmallows and drank homemade hot cocoa while we talked about friendship.

Doc started it. He lifted his mug and said, "A toast to you... our friend now and ever."

"Here, here!" Gus said in his deep voice. Emma and Jake chimed in. We all drank a swallow and Doc said the best quote about friendship was by Albert Camus: "Don't walk behind me; I may not lead. Don't walk in front of me; I may not follow. Just walk beside me and be my friend."

"You're the finest friends I've ever had in my whole life," I said. "I wish I could put it into words." And one by one, they put it into words for me.

"Acquaintances are plentiful, but true friends are rare," Emma said. "I think a friend is that person who loves you, warts and all. They don't wanna change you, rearrange you, fix you, or make you into their idea of 'better.' In their eyes, you're perfect, just like you are." We all nodded and murmured our agreements. Then, she held up a waggling pointer finger. "But!" she said dramatically, "there are two times when that changes. First, if you ask for help in order to become more of yourself, a friend'll stand right beside you, encouragin' and pushin' and supportin' your growin' with all their might. Second, if a friend sees you fallin' apart or, as Carlie says, 'circlin' the drain,' and you can't ask for help or are so troubled you won't, a real friend'll dive down that drain to save you."

That touched me. It touched us all.

Next Gus said, "I ain't thought afore on this friendship thing. I jes' did for folks or they did for me. But what I've seen with y'all was somethin' I thought I'd only have with Emma here. Trust. I'd trust any of ya." He looked at Doc, then me, then Jake. "I'd trust ya with my life. I'd trust ya with my home, my harvest, and my sweet Emma. If'n somethin' happened to me, I know all of you would show up for her and love her even more 'n you already do. Y'all know love's a verb. And you demonstrate it right fine." He paused, looking into the fire, then turned to us, smiling. "It's trust and it makes you feel safe... that's what friendship is." He nodded his head firmly once, the period at the end of his sentence.

Jake shifted on his lawn chair, gazing into the fire. "I have not thought of friendship as you do." He paused in his usual fashion, considering the weight of the words he would carefully use. "My understanding of this thing with people is small, but great in a different way.

"I am honored by countless friends—every plant harvested is my friend that gives its healing medicine. It wouldn't have given it otherwise. Mother Earth is my friend, the rocks and dirt, the clay and stones. Father Sky, night stars, thunder and wind... rushing water, high deserts, and the beetle on a thistle stem." He paused again. "Pinon nuts that fall to the ground to feed us, every fish, graceful deer, great warrior owl that hunts by night... and small black cats are all my friends.

"We are connected, each thing a part of every other thing. I am friends with all inhabitants of nature that live their lives honorably and with purpose." We thought he was done speaking, then he added one more thing, "To be the friend of man or woman is also such an honor." He looked at Doc. "For me, to call someone 'friend' is the same as 'Water Brothers.' A friend is a commitment for life." He looked into our eyes, one by one. "You honor me with your friendship," he said, and I saw a painful beauty in his face I will never forget.

Then we looked at Doc.

He rose and warmed his hands for a few moments over the dying embers of the fire pit, then turned to face us. "I was privileged to spend significant time learning about friendship at a level I didn't know existed. MJ and Cochon taught me. I learned that once in a while we meet someone we are so inexplicably drawn to that it feels like divine intervention. When that happens, there is a confluence, a connection that it is so strong it is hard to imagine it not existing—as if the rising of the sun depends on it. This is what I saw between those two cats. It came in a hundred different demonstrations; acceptance of the other, keen interest, admiration, respect for each other's different strengths and frailties.

"I heard stories from each of you about MJ's patience and acceptance of Cochon before the miracle of his growth happened. MJ didn't push or berate or reject. He met Cochon where he lived, inside his small, fearful world where the door to life was cracked but not open. I heard how, through love and patience, trust was born. How MJ's ability to be fully feline and fully alive awoke something in Cochon. This is friendship in its purest. And MJ only led until Cochon could walk on his own. Then they were equals, with an easy give and take that left both without the need to be first or best or most important." He uncrossed his legs and leaned forward, elbows on knees.

"I am so touched by the privilege I was granted to be a tiny part of their lives." I saw wetness under his eyes. He didn't wipe it away or explain it. "Caring for them gave me multiple opportunities to feel awe and wonder. My awareness of the mystical quality of life was made richer and more precious." And I thought how I wasn't the only one who had been made more aware of life's enchantment.

"I experienced something beautiful, and felt such joy and humility watching them." He was quiet a few moments, then looked at us, smiling. "Because of the Water Brothers, I am able to be a better friend to each of you, a better father, a better doctor. I am thoroughly thankful for that."

I think we were all a little teary-eyed at that point. We sat quietly, listening to the crackling of the fire and shifting of the embers. Then Emma said, "I just can't cry one more drop. I think a little music is in order." She hurried inside and returned with her new boom box and a cassette tape of Three Dog Night. She turned it on, and to everyone's surprise, began to sway and sing the words to "Try A Little Tenderness."

"Come on, you lazy coot!" she said, pulling Gus from his chair. He grumbled something but slipped his arm around her waist so naturally, and we watched, entranced, as they danced in their work shoes under New Mexico stars.

Shortly afterward, we all hugged again and went our separate ways. I walked back to the house and was warmed by two sweet faces in the window; my friends waiting for me.

⌇

My sister and brother arrived the next day in the morning. We swung by the U-Haul center and rented the truck. My brother drove it back to Bosque Farms, following my sister and I in the car. Jake and Doc showed up that afternoon with Barry and Sissy Mackland, and Carol and Dave to help pack the truck. It took less than two hours. That night, Emma cooked, and we ate together in a merry group filled with conversation and laughter. Once, I looked up and saw her looking at me with such a sweet smile I had to walk outside and cry. *Again.* For the umpteenth time. She found me by their garage, sniffing away, and told me this was the nature of life. It had to keep moving. At that moment, I just wanted it to stay still.

My brother was thrilled to sleep at Gus and Emma's on their large bed in the guest room. Sis and I slept at my house on an air mattress on the floor, the cats finding solace amid the confusion, cuddling between us as I breathed in the cool night air of my last New Mexico night.

The following cloudless morning, after Emma's homemade burritos and cinnamon buns, we drove away at ten. She had packed us lunches and snacks. My brother asked, "Who *are* these people?!" as he peeked into his bulging lunch sack.

Before we turned the corner, I looked back and Emma stood alone, still waving.

Deidre and Cochon were in separate carriers in the back seat. Mostly Deidre voiced her disapproval of the moving car situation, though Cochon chimed in occasionally for support. By the time we were on 40 East, they had settled into the moment and dozed.

My sister drove and I was thankful. I was too weepy and tired. Entering Missouri, I saw a pond of standing water in a farmer's field. Several miles down the road, there was a bigger pond. Then another. And another. I had lived with such dry weather conditions in the Southwest that standing water existed only because it would be used. I marveled at these indiscriminate, seemingly unneeded small treasures. Sis asked what I was looking at.

"Water... for no reason. Unused, just sitting there," I said, shaking my head at the wealth of liquid gold. I had forgotten how plentiful and rich this part of the country was in its water bounty.

I started saying, "Water, for no reason," every time we passed water, small or large. I said it so often, I shortened it to an abbreviation: water F.N.R. I pronounced it "finner."

Then she started saying it. "Look, there on the left! Water finner!" It was just silliness, but it lifted my mood. At one point, we both laughed so hard we cried. And within moments, mine turned into a different cry as every mile took me further from my heart's true home. More release. As Doc said, it would take time...

We followed my brother's expert lead and arrived in Illinois two and a half days later. I had left my home and come to another home. I had left everything I loved in New Mexico and come back to the first people I loved in this life. I had come full circle.

Mom met me at the door, Dad supporting her as he firmly held her right elbow, his other arm securely around her back as she listed toward him. She wanted to stand to welcome me home, not sit in the wheelchair that waited behind her. She cried as I hugged her thin body. I cried too, but the tears were sweet, not salty, and the pain was intertwined with joy.

That night, I slept in my childhood bedroom. *How did so many children fit in this house?* The next day, while my brother and his friends unloaded furniture and boxes into storage, I went with mom to physical therapy. She had such grace and dignity as she concentrated on the small tests they gave her.

One of the PT women spoke very loudly and talked down to her like she was a child. Mom smiled, reached out for the woman's hand and said softly, "The stroke didn't affect my hearing, so you can speak quieter. And I'm sure you're not aware you're doing it, but you talk down to me and it hurts. I need confidence right now." The woman looked surprised. Mom squinted to read her name badge. "And Jerri, I am a few hours short of a doctorate and still have all my faculties, so I understand your instructions perfectly well. I hope you don't mind that I'm honest with you. I know you can be *such* a great help to me." I saw the woman melt. Of course she didn't mind.

My brother returned to his home a couple hours away, and my sister and I ate with Mom and Dad that night. I cooked Enchilada Chicken Casserole, and they found it delicious. Emma had sent home-canned apple butter, green chili salsa, and a couple loaves of horno oven bread. I found myself talking a lot about my home and friends. I was homesick already.

But here I was, and here I was determined to be at peace with the many moments that made each day. I couldn't go backwards. There was only now and the road I would walk.

Epilogue

The Final Miracle

"The wound is the place where the Light enters you."
– Rumi

Time changes everything, whether I pay attention or not. It changes people and bodies, decisions and understandings. It changes cities and politics and the course of rivers. It changes seasons.

In the fall, a year after I moved home, we buried my mother. Confused cells began to replicate into what is called cancer. She had become tired, and food lost its savor. She lost weight, slept a lot, and when the tests came back, the doctor said it was all over her body, even in her brain. *Absolutely not. Mistakes are made in hospitals all the time.* But I flinched at the sound of crunching fall leaves underfoot as I left hospice for the last time. I had traversed this sidewalk countless times during her last few days. Walking on the dry leaves was an audial cue that never failed to instantly bring up the loss and pain of her dying. I didn't like fall for several years.

When my mother died that dark, rainy evening in hospice, my father got lost. How did one go on without their polestar? He disengaged inside, and we never truly found him again. He walked like a ghost in the big house, looking for something he could never find.

I experienced my own loss of reality. Deidre and Cochon became glued to my side as they sensed my pain. But there was nothing anyone could do. She was gone. My siblings and I couldn't quite be there for each other—we were all lost in our own pain and didn't have the strength to take on more. We each grieved alone. But in the end, perhaps grieving is something we do alone, anyway.

My New Mexico friends cried with me on the phone. They cried in their hearts as they felt life's minutes ticking by, reminding them we were all going to leave one day. They cried without tears as they held a sacred space for me over the many miles, a safe place to talk and ask and not know. I gave myself to the grief as I had with MJ, allowing the tears to come whenever they wanted, without judging. I thought I grieved in a healthy way. But just when I felt an equilibrium establish, I would spend time with my father or siblings, and it would shudder and fall apart all over again.

I had moved into the guest house behind my parents' home shortly after arriving from New Mexico. They owned six acres of land and Dad mowed the one acre around the buildings. It looked like a park. Attached on one corner of that acre was the rest of their five acres—what my parents had laughingly called "The Lower 40." That land was only mowed enough to make a wide swath to the edge of their brushy, old-growth forest. It was a magical place, and I would go there often to be alone. The cats joined me, and sometimes Cochon would stay long after I left, sitting quietly, just looking into the jewelweed and black raspberry bushes that grew in wild abandon below the old trees.

One early evening, over a year after Mom died, I sat on the four seasons porch—my watching and thinking place—and stared into the woods beyond the house. I loved coming out here at dawn and dusk to watch the animals that called this land home: birds, slinky foxes, porcupines, skunks, racoons, coyotes, and deer. Lately, I always brought the new phone, a modern invention that was cordless and even displayed the number of the person calling. I started keeping it beside me so I could be quickly available if Dad fell or got confused and needed something.

When it rang and I saw Doc's number, I was overjoyed. Though we talked every few weeks, each time felt special. He asked about the cats. Deidre was her usual loving self, but Cochon seemed to be pulling away a little. He spent more time out roaming than he had in Bosque Farms. He also seemed to be more tired when he returned. His eating, coat, and gum color were normal, so he asked me to keep him informed. I told Doc he was like my dad—he had lost his polestar.

When he asked about me, I started to cry. Through my tears and runny nose, I told him I just cried too much. A little thing would set me off... a song my mom and I sang, a commercial with old people in it, the smell of morning coffee reminding me of countless cups we had shared on my porch. And the many times I saw something in a store or on TV or in a book and thought, *Mom is gonna love this*, before realizing in the next second that she wasn't here to love anything ever again.

Doc assured me these were normal experiences. "We all grieve in different ways," he said. "The most important thing is to understand the value of grief. Your heart has a wound. Whether it's a cut on your body or a cut on your heart, wounds weep. On bodies it's called serous fluid. On hearts it's called tears. It is healing to cry, just like it's healing on a cut finger for it to weep a while."

"But it's been over a year, Doc," I said, wiping my nose. "Shouldn't all this crying and grieving be over by now?"

"Who said?" he asked. "A book? Someone on TV? A friend? There's no standard of how long a person should grieve. If you quit comparing yourself to what you think is normal, stop judging every tear and quit being embarrassed by them, you'll get along much better. If you welcome grief in and accept it for what it is—a gift of healing—it will eventually transform. It will change from an 'I shouldn't be crying again–I'm a mess–what's wrong with me' moment into loving memories without the pain attached. No one knows how long each person will take to heal. Be patient with yourself."

Another year passed, and one afternoon I looked into Cochon's face and noticed a pinched look around his eyes. The next day, I watched him slowly return home in the cold from The Lower 40, and his usually luxurious, fluffy coat looked too flat. He was still grooming attentively, but the Knower got my attention. I took him to the vet's.

After tests, she told me his kidney values were off and to bring him back in a couple weeks to test again. But he began to decline quickly, and I took him back four days later. She said his kidneys were failing. Did he get into leaked anti-freeze? she wondered. I didn't know; he roamed where he wanted to, but I doubted it. Our cars didn't leak, and we only had two neighbors. He never wandered by their homes or onto the street.

She gave him 100 cc of normal saline just under his skin around the back of his neck where his shoulder blades met. He perked up. He seemed relieved and had more energy for a few days, running outside on the brown grass, climbing trees, and chasing Deidre through the house. But it didn't last, and he was back for fluids at the vet's weekly for a couple months.

The time came when she recommended he be given the sub-cutaneous IVs twice a week and taught me to do it at home. Doc sent me a tincture of alfalfa from a New Mexico apothecary to give him—a couple drops daily. It helped, and IVs returned to once a week for several months.

It was in that Spring that I discovered he could only go halfway to The Lower 40 before he sat down, unable to continue. I picked him up and carried him there in my arms. We sat together watching the tiny wrens, jeweled butterflies, and the tree limbs swaying smoothly like slow-motion hula dancers. On a carpet of thick

Kentucky bluegrass, we listened to sounds of birds and bullfrogs, fat bees, and cars passing a long way off on the highway.

Sometimes I meditated as Doc had shown me, my body still and relaxed as my mind followed its lead. Occasionally, brilliant pictures would show up, unbidden. This day, it showed a tiny movie of Cochon and MJ playing a game of chase around the adobe house in Bosque Farms, their bodies moving like dancing panthers, their joy palpable. When I opened my eyes, Cochon had laid down on his side facing me, his paws contracting, letting go, contracting, letting go, like he and MJ used to do when they mirrored each other. I'll never know in what way or how much he missed his Water Brother.

After the sun moved behind a bank of trees, I asked him, "Ready to go back?" He sat up, wobbled to one side, then got his footing. I picked him up and carried him the long way home where Deidre waited for us by the door.

Within a month, I was giving him a subcutaneous IV every two days. He wasn't eating much and drank copious amounts of water. His once glorious fur coat became dark and greasy looking. He slept a lot with Deidre, and they still cuddled, intertwined so close that I couldn't tell in the dark where one ended and the other began.

I consulted with Doc, and he asked how I felt about euthanasia. "You mean, am I okay with someone else killing him?" I asked bluntly.

He paused, then said, "Yes. That's what I'm asking. I won't pretend to imagine I know what he's feeling physically, let alone emotionally. But the fact that his coat is quite dirty, he has quit eating and grooming, sleeps most of the time, and drinks too much water says what to you?"

"That he's dying." A sob tore at my chest as I choked, unwilling to release the wail in my heart. Doc was quiet, letting my own words reverberate in the silence.

Later that morning, Cochon had a seizure. His little body jerked, and he step-hopped sideways and slammed into the wall. He fell on his side and stiffened, his feet kicked and kicked, and he foamed at the mouth. He made himself get up, only to go through the same thing all over again. It lasted maybe three minutes but felt like three heart-wrenching hours. I was deeply shaken when it finally stopped. I called the vet and she and her assistant came to the house that evening. And, of course, by then he seemed fine. He had eaten a little dinner, played softly with Deidre and fell sound asleep with her on the couch. I almost turned the vet away.

She said his kidneys were so poor at doing their job that the toxicity levels in his body must be extremely high. Seizures were the end stage of kidney disease. This was the sole thing I dreaded about bringing an animal into my life and heart: that I may at some point have to become the arbiter of its life or death.

At 5:56pm, Cochon breathed his last breath.

I covered him with a soft towel and left him on the floor of the living room on a mat. I wanted Deidre to be able to read his story with her nose, like she'd done with MJ. She sat beside him for brief periods off and on, then finally disappeared to a corner of the room to watch. Later, I ran a shallow bath, gently laid him in the warm water and lovingly washed his greasy fur, dirty feet, cleaned his ears, and rinsed him well. I sang the song about Ho'zho' ... "Beauty all around, beauty all around, beauty all around..." and it calmed me. Then, I used the blow dryer to brush and dry his fur. He was beautiful, the color of Female Rain again, even though it covered a bony landscape. Once again, he looked like my beautiful boy.

I set his body on a small table, covered with a big scarf I had purchased in Madrid, New Mexico. It was all the colors of Talavera pottery, mixed with a thousand sunsets. I picked spring flowers and placed them beside him, along with his favorite toy. I called people who had loved him or had only met him and told them he would be here for two more days if they wanted to say goodbye. Several did. Each brought a sympathy card, and a couple brought more flowers. No one left with dry eyes.

My dad, sister, and I dug a hole in the yard against a fence by the blueberry bushes. I didn't have a beautiful wooden box, so I used one of my mother's embroidered pillowcases. We all shared a memory. To this day, I don't recall what any of us said, but I do remember we sang "I'll Be Loving You Always," one of my mom's favorite songs. We sang it to him, choking and sputtering as we tried to harmonize. I put Cochon's two favorite mouse toys beside him, along with a plastic bag with a photo of Deidre—the mother who adopted him, his lifelong friend, his constant. Next to Deidre's picture, I placed another plastic bag with the only picture I had of MJ.

MJ: his Water Brother, his friend, his teacher who had given him his very best, then had left him to navigate the world on his own.

Deidre and I uncomfortably settled into a different life. It was a painful life for a while. I couldn't comfort her, and she couldn't comfort me. It reminded me of Emma's description of her and Gus after their son, Ronnie, died. "We were like two ghosts that couldn't see each other. We did things together but were miles apart."

Deidre and I still slept together in the same bed, ate breakfast and dinner in the same kitchen, but in between meals she would disappear, and I'd find her outside wandering aimlessly or staring into the forest. My heart broke for her. I remember feeling like I had failed them all.

I railed at myself. *You didn't do enough for MJ, Mom, or Cochon. If you had only checked sooner, demanded less, asked for more, been more attentive, interfered less, been more relaxed, been less relaxed, not been so worried, been more worried... What's* wrong *with you!*

I got no answer. I regretted all my decisions. I carried guilt for the choices I had and hadn't made.

Sometimes I railed at God. *You take goodness out of the world and leave evil—what kind of sense does* that *make? You take three of the kindest, sweetest beings on Earth and let them die, while you let murderers and child molesters and the most vile people on Earth live. What's* wrong *with you?* I got no answer.

I had to wait over a week to be able to call Doc. I needed time to quit spraying the world with anger and tears and sorrow. When we finally connected, he listened. I told him that I knew I had failed them all: MJ, Mom, Cochon.

"I didn't know you were that powerful." His words startled me out of my haze of self-flagellation. *What did he mean, powerful? I just said I'd let them all down. That's powerless, not powerful.* He continued, "If you failed them, that means you think you could have controlled the outcomes of three lives. And that is another way of saying you have the power over life and death. Like I said, I didn't know you were that powerful." I grappled with his words.

He continued, "And if you have that kind of power, then you abdicated your power and left it up to the whim of circumstance. So, if you indeed had the power of life and death and didn't exercise it, then I agree... you failed them all."

I didn't say anything for the longest time, and he didn't interrupt the silence. Several minutes later, I asked him something I had never asked before. "What do I do? Of course I don't have the power to control life and death, but even realizing how ridiculous my statement is doesn't stop the bleeding inside. I don't know what will. What do I do, Doc?"

I heard him change his position in the chair he occupied over a thousand miles away. "Do you remember me sharing with you that grief was a wound of the heart and to let the wound weep?" I told him I remembered it well. "It seems, dear one, that the wound has gotten some dirt in it. As long as it's dirty, it will be infected and never heal."

Then, he said four little words I'll never forget, words so innocuous I could have easily dismissed them. "Keep the wound clean," he said. Though I didn't understand fully, I glimpsed a rightness to his words that felt like Truth with a capital "T." He continued.

"The only thing that can dirty up a wound of the heart is guilt. Or you might call it regret. Have you had thoughts that say you should have done more or better or different about the three loves you've lost?"

I smiled and asked, "Are you reading my mind now?" We both chuckled.

"As long as you believe you could have done something different, it remains your fault that the cats and your mother died. As long as you beat yourself up because you should have thought or done or spoken or felt differently, it's your fault.

"As long as you think this, you will cry. If you don't remove the dirt, for the rest of your days you will feel guilty and beat yourself up with all the things you 'should' have done. You'll still feel responsible and broken-hearted on your deathbed."

He stopped and took a gentle breath. "You weren't responsible. You did what you thought was best with the light and understanding you had. No one can ask for more. Let the regret and guilt go so you can heal. Can you do that?"

I told him I would work on it.

I started paying close attention to the thoughts that had gained traction, including the voice that said I should have watched Cochon more carefully when he went outside, the one that shamed me for not being a good steward of his precious life, the voice that searched for clues I had missed as to his well-being, and the voice that said similar things about MJ and my own mother. I watched the thoughts pass by. They weren't me. They were just thoughts that swirled around inside my brain like refuse circling a drain.

As I began to feel better, I ignored the seductive voice that said, "But I have to be real! I can't pretend to feel happy and good! I have to be miserable!" This whining, pouty voice wasn't who I was. I began to hear the many thoughts as passing traffic on the street, and I let go and let go and let go, over and over again.

The thoughts would disappear for a few days, then I would hear them again, wanting to punish me for all my past failures. But each time they were softer and quieter and with less strength. Then, they became so soft they were but mere whispers, and one day, I noticed that even though they arrived and spoke their lies, I felt nothing. No guilt, no regret, only love and sweetness for those I had lost.

I returned to focusing my attention outward and poured it into Deidre who was more devastated than I had known. She and I spent hours together. I began taking her to Dad's house when I took care of him. He fell in love, but who couldn't fall in love with Deidre? She ate better, slept better, and groomed better. But she was lonely. Sometimes she would cry over and over, her meows full of questions. I held her, brushed her, talked with her, but I couldn't fill in for Cochon. I was just a human.

A cool morning in September, three months after we'd buried Cochon, I sat on the porch and she joined me. "I think it's time you had some companionship, sweet girl." She hopped onto my lap and began to knead, purring. I smoothed her head and back until she hopped off. I found a listing for the humane society in the phone directory, dug the carrier out of the closet, grabbed a couple towels, and drove to the shelter, arriving just as it opened.

I told them I wanted a kitten. Deidre was the best surrogate mother Cochon could have ever wanted, and a new kitten would give her purpose. The shelter only had one, a coal black, tiny thing that meowed loudly when I picked it up. I asked for its history, how many siblings it had, how old it was, and they didn't know. It had been dropped off that morning at their door in a paper bag, stapled shut at the top. It included a note that just said, "Can't keep him." He was a short-haired male with a bucketful of kitteny cuteness. The little kitten and I drove home, stopping by the grocery store to pick up kitten food.

When we arrived, Deidre was lounging on the bed. I set the carrier on the floor and the kitten began to talk. Deidre watched, then carefully got down and sniffed the carrier, especially the door where she could see the little one inside. She looked at me, rather wide-eyed, as if to say, "What the heck is this?"

"I brought you a friend, honey. Shall we let him out to explore? You ready?" She ignored me, so I opened the carrier. The kitten sniffed and sniffed, then went up to Deidre and started nudging her side, like it was looking for milk. Deidre scampered away and hopped back up on the bed to watch. I took the little guy into the kitchen and gave him kitten food, which he devoured with typical kitten gusto.

That night he woke us up over and over. He wanted to sleep with us but was too unsure of himself. How would he get down to use the litter box? In the middle of the night, I got up and positioned boxes and suitcases to create makeshift steps. After that, we slept until he woke us again around five, crying for food. He was noisy, as some kittens are, and very energetic.

By the end of that first day, I began to think of him as odd. I could see why the first people returned him. He didn't walk, he ran. He jumped repeatedly, as if he saw something above him and had to jump for it. But there was nothing to grab, but air. I put away his makeshift stairs after a couple days when he started running from the living room to the bedroom at top speed to claw his way up the bedding to reach the top. He looked like a monkey, all arms and legs going in impossible directions.

He began to climb the walls. He would run at top speed, then take off like a fighter jet, jumping as high as he could onto the wall. Then, he would literally climb a few inches until he turned the top half of his body around and would jump off. Midair he would twist, land on his feet, then look at me or Deidre with a crazed look before taking off into another room. The look reminded me of Jack Nicholson in *The Shining*.

He scared me a little. I began to wonder if cats could be possessed. Or mentally imbalanced. When my sister came over to visit, she watched him for a while, then turned to me, wide-eyed. "There's something not right about that little guy," she said. "He's climbing the dang walls. How does he even *do* that?"

"I don't know," I told her. "I think the textured plaster must be soft enough that his tiny claws dig in and keep him going." I shook my head. Deidre came over to sit on my lap. I stroked and massaged and rubbed her head and back to her tail. Sis reached out and cooed how beautiful she was. Deidre basked in the attention.

"How are they getting along?" she asked.

I hated to admit it. I didn't want to give up on this crazy kitten. "They're not," I said, shaking my head. "She can't stand him. And I don't blame her. He jumps right on top of her while she's sleeping. Then he gets this wide-eyed, goofy look on his face as if to say, 'I'm baaack!' and she hisses at him, jumps off the bed, and hides. The other day, I found her sleeping on the kitchen counter, the only place he couldn't reach her."

"That's not good," my sister said, watching him run from room to room, then climb the cat trees, then the drapes.

"No!" I said in my "no voice" that had trained countless cats in the past. He heard it and froze, whipping his head back to look at me. I walked over and loosened his claws from the drapery and put him down. Then I sat down on the floor and scooped him up onto my lap, whispering and cooing as I massaged his tiny body. He began to relax and finally fell asleep on his back.

That night I was hopeful... until he startled us both out of a deep sleep to scamper across our heads. Repeatedly. After his tiny form finally dozed off, I talked silently to MJ, hoping wherever he was he could hear me. "MJ? Please help us. Give him some strength, some peace. Help him find his balance in this world." My heart ached.

He had been with us a week now and I still hadn't named him. I finally chose his everyday name as "Rumi," after my favorite mystic poet. The poetry was wild and full of passion, but also gentle and kind and full of love. If this little kitten could grow into that state of beingness, he would handle life quite well. Also, I read Rumi was a Sufi, a whirling dervish. It seemed a good reminder as I watched him blindly twirl in the air before landing. I hoped that energy could be contained and directed, not just splattered all over the place.

But Rumi kept making life miserable for Deidre. He continued to climb the walls and jump and whirl midair, his energy making the true dervishes look lazy by comparison. It helped him when I began leaving the door to the screened-in porch open. Outside, he had much more stimulation and began to sit in the cat tree and watch the outside world. Deidre had some time without his constant pestering and was able to nap without interruption once in a while. But he still acted like he had a screw loose.

My dad came over for coffee one morning and told me he thought he was nuts and I should take him for a brain scan. Instead, for the thousandth time, I wished MJ was here to show me what to do. But MJ was gone, gone with the thousands of white snow geese. Gone without ever letting me know he was okay.

I was lost as to how to help the small, black kitten who didn't rest enough or calm down enough, or even exhibit a tiny bit of belonging. It was as if he was always running away from something and couldn't run fast enough.

Though Dad thought he should be taken back, he also gave assurances Rumi would "grow out of it." Each day, when I went over to his house, he would ask how the crazy one was doing.

I was in and out at Dad's, but typically showed up to help him cook dinner. We were all afraid he would leave the fire on under a pan, something that had happened twice. We chopped vegetables together and made salads and cooked meat or eggs, pasta or stir-fry. Sometimes I ate with him, sometimes not.

One evening, I had finished a pot of spaghetti and told him I was tired. Rumi had awakened us every hour since two that morning. So, I served Dad his food, got a bowl for myself, and went home.

I didn't see Rumi on the porch, so I went inside to feed all of us dinner. Deidre came immediately, but not the little black kitten. I looked through the house. Nothing. I opened closet doors, calling him, but there wasn't the tiniest rustle. I went back to the porch and checked the screens, looking for holes in them. Nothing. Then I moved the heavy cat tree and found a small rip in the screen. It was just big enough to get a two-pound kitten through.

Panicked, I grabbed the flashlight. Outside was pitch black, and home to foxes and coyotes that would make a snack out of the tiny newcomer. I pushed the fear aside and turned on the outside porch-light, calling him. "Rumi! Here, kitty, kitty, kitty!" I tried to sound calm as I called repeatedly, walking the full perimeter around the house. I shined the flashlight into the bushes out back, sure I'd find him. Nothing again. Then, off to the side of the house I heard the smallest sound. I steadied the light and slowly panned the grassy area about thirty feet away.

That was when I saw him.

But what I saw made chills run down my back and stop my breath.

Rumi was dancing in a circle around a tall, black cat that sat motionless, staring at me. It had bright copper eyes that shone like burnished pennies off the flashlight's beam.

MJ?

Its right ear was chewed, and its right leg had a white stripe on it that ran from shoulder to paw. *No... no, no, it can't be...* There was a small crescent moon-shaped bit of skin showing on its left cheek. *How...?*

It was MJ. But it couldn't be MJ. He'd been dead over three years, killed on a rainy country road and buried under a great oak tree in New Mexico.

I can't fully describe what happened next, but something called out to me, "Shhhh! Look!" with such force that it seemed to come from everywhere. And with all of me, I looked.

He was glorious, his big, noble head held high. The flashlight glistened off his rich, black coat. MJ was here. His calm presence emanated peace and, strangely, a kind of mirth, as if he wanted me to know this dying thing wasn't such a big deal after all.

MJ was here. Looking at me, looking *into* me, reminding me of things it seemed I had known long ago before I could speak, things perhaps I was born knowing but had forgotten. I will never find the right words to share what I experienced because they haven't been created yet.

But in the few paltry words I can find, I will tell you what I understood. He was reminding me... that all is well, that life is a dance of magical particles that form all things—things that remind us of what we are and what exquisite joy there is in our aliveness that never ends. He reminded me this was but one experience in a fathomless well of experiences. How sweetly it all can be held and used and released! And he reminded me that love was the force behind our lives as it whispered and pushed and nudged us toward the Creator within and without. He reminded me that what I really was, was the essence under the personality. MJ was here to share a glimpse of what he knew and the peace he felt.

As our eyes stayed locked, I sensed more than reminders. He had brought me a gift: a message that we go on, that this life isn't fatal, that we live just as we have always lived... *forever.* I was life and life was me. We are eternal and he wanted me to remember.

Click.

I continued to look into his copper eyes as a tsunami-size wave of understanding washed between us. From the shores of his heart to the shores of mine, it drenched me in peace. In that moment, we shared the sweetest love and thankfulness. All he had done for Cochon! All he had done for all of us in Bosque Farms. And now all he was doing for Rumi.

Suddenly, MJ blinked and Cochon's face filled my mind, and I knew MJ had been with him. As sure as I breathed, I knew they had been together down in The Lower 40. The Water Brothers had filled each other up as they always had.

All of this came without words. I don't know how I comprehended these things. I just did.

MJ was also here for something else. How many times had I wished he was alive to help bring peace to such an unsettled, little kitten? I sensed he was giving something to Rumi, something unseen and pure. Days later, I would think of it as a blessing. The MJ blessing.

Suddenly, Rumi stopped and reached out a tiny paw to touch MJ's strong thigh. And like a benediction, the great black cat bent down and licked the top of the little kitten's head. Rumi accepted his gentle lick and then turned in a circle and continued to jump and twirl and dance, over and over again. Just then, my dad opened his front door and called out, "I heard you calling the cat. Is everything okay?"

I turned my head for a fraction of a second—a mere fraction—and called, "It's okay. Got him." He grunted and closed the door.

When I turned quickly back, MJ was gone.

I washed the lawn with the flashlight back and forth, looking for him. I knew he had accomplished what he wanted to do here and was gone. But I didn't want him to go. I wanted him to stay forever. Because *he* was forever.

Rumi still pranced in the dark, but now he jumped at fireflies that peppered the August night. I walked over and picked him up. I started to turn away, then shone the flashlight onto the grass where MJ had sat. It was slightly flattened. I reached down to touch it with my hand and there was a mild warmth. Chills ran through my arm into my whole body.

What did I just witness? What just happened here? I heard Carlita's sweet, high voice from years ago whisper, "Es un milagro."

MJ had brought the first miracle for Cochon. Now he brought another miracle for Rumi, though I wasn't sure what it was. Until later...

That night, for the first time since the little black tornado had come to live with us, we all slept peacefully. If either cat got up, I never knew, because both were quiet and went back to sleep. He didn't wake me in the morning, either. I woke up on my own to find him lounging in the cat tree on the porch, watching the birds. That morning, Rumi ran and jumped, but not on Deidre. He was energetic, but not crazed. He played with his toys and climbed the

242

cat perch, but he didn't climb the walls. He never climbed them again.

Something magical had been given to the tiny kitten. Something that spoke to his spirit. After his ecstatic whirling and dancing around MJ, he changed. He became a playful, yet peaceful kitten, no matter how rambunctious he was. As if a switch had been flicked, suddenly he could relax, his tight ball of a body lengthening to stretch and reach out to softly touch Deidre or me or a blade of grass.

From that day on, Rumi was an amazing kitten who transformed over the years into a wise and kind teacher for so many others. He became a leader and protector, a great hunter who walked like a panther and loved like a Water Brother. He walked in beauty.

That warm August night he had received something from MJ that had healed him.

And, as had been the case so many times before, I had too.

October 2022

Gentle Reader...

Thank you for taking time to read my book! I hope you found it a force for good in your life. It was started over twenty years ago and gathered dust until one day it whispered, "Will you *please* finish me, for heaven's sake?!" Finally, it went out into the world and into hands. I am thrilled it made it into yours.

If you enjoyed this book, please consider making the book more visible by leaving an honest review on Amazon, Goodreads, Barnes and Noble, or the site of your choice. Reviews shine the light!

Authors *love* feedback. Email me at tian@tianwilson.com. I answer every email personally and look forward to meeting you. And check out my website at www.tianwilson.com for a free gift!

Again, thank you from the bottom of my heart,

Tian

Acknowledgments

It takes a village to wake up a book, stand it on its legs, get it all spruced up, shoes on, face washed, hair combed, and send it forth into the world. I am deeply grateful to each person who contributed in any way to help it walk into its life.

Lynn Underwood was the catalyst for this book. There was so much pushing and encouraging and nudging until I wanted to yell, "Stop, already!" But I didn't. When I read the first chapter aloud, you believed this was a book to be shared, not a story to be ignored as it slept and dreamed in a dusty, ten-year old folder. You continued to push me—right toward someone who understood procrastinators. Thanks to Jeanne Johansen for valuing the beauty of a deadline.

Once awake, it was time to stand it on its legs. So, the Brothers Underwood brought Mustang Sally into the creative process. Where would I be without her? I'll forever thank you both for the peace of mind that gave to me.

Part of the village were those who used their considerable expertise to keep an eye on the facts. I especially thank Dr. Todd Webster, veterinarian extraordinaire. Thank you for your wisdom and hours of discussion on procedures that bring our furry friends back to wellness. Your kindness and compassion, your extensive knowledge of how to treat animals holistically as well as allopathically, was instrumental to the story. Even more, you believe the miracles happened—high endorsement from a vet.

Another fact-checker was Tom Smylie, one of the world's top falconers and a long-time naturalist in New Mexico. Thanks, Tom, for ensuring that references to the geography, flora, and fauna were accurate. And that the winged creatures of the sky had their story told honestly. Your deep understanding of New Mexico and your love of birds and the lands they inhabit brought another dimension to this special book.

Marc Adams, psychologist, therapist, lover of Jung and all things sane, was there when the writing began to circle the drain. You helped strengthen my own ideas with your insightful questions and comments, and helped me remember some of the wisdom I thought I'd forgotten.

How can I ever duly thank my other New Mexico friends? Maureen Doherty who offered encouragement along with ideas and facts about Bosque Farms—you awoke memories I had forgotten. Without your idea of my renting your sister's home, this story would have never happened. A little serendipity...

And gratitude for Therese and Ed Sims. Who spends a day taking pictures in Bosque Farms to remind me of textures, sights, and sounds? You did. I so wished I could have smelled the fields and farms with you as you drove the back roads through the little village.

A special thank you to Dr. Pamellina Cornish who sent cheers and hurrahs, cards, and you-can-do-its along with occasional presents for the writer, ever cheering me on to the finish line. You made each milestone a celebration, my friend.

And last, blessings of grace were received from my Diné friends. You graciously gave me a glimpse of your beautiful world. Though you want to remain anonymous, your names ring in my heart.

As the little book prepared to enter the world, my Beta Readers stepped in to scrub its face. My deepest appreciation to all of you who took the time to read, consider, answer questions, and pen comments. Marc Adams, Craig Gundry, Debra Henderson, Liz Hill, Heather Miller, Cathy Pratt, Robert Schultz, Tom Smylie, Todd Webster, and others who don't want accolades, not only showed me the smudges I missed, but offered bounteous support and inspiration. *Gifts From a Feral Cat* wouldn't be what it is without your perceptive ideas and feedback.

Dustin Bilyk, of The Author's Hand, and I were strangers a month ago. Now you are my mentor, copyeditor, and "Professional Nudger." Your copyediting and formatting ensured the book's hair was combed. I deeply appreciate your patience, word prowess, and sense of humor. Even more, I appreciate you reading the whole book to give me your honest assessment and encouragement. You handed the little book its jacket after you smoothed the wrinkles out and plucked the lint off the seams.

Glory be to those with an artistic eye! Thank you, Craig Gundry, for creating the book cover that makes people want to go inside and join the characters. You beautifully captured the sights, colors, and spirit of The Land of Enchantment. You have spread a banquet for the eyes as you addressed every detail, no matter how small. Your artwork imparts a sense of wistfulness and beauty to accompany this timeless story.

Two people in my family repeatedly said it was time to finish this book, which had languished half done for over a decade. Thank you to my sweet and bigger-than-life cousin, Brett. The family storyteller, you ensured I would grow up loving a good tale. When you heard part of the story a decade ago and said there was a book inside my "lyrical prose," my heart sang. Thank you for never failing to ask in your booming voice, "How's the book coming?" I think you knew I could do this before I did.

The other person was my sister, Cathy. You were the first one I called when the final miracle occurred those oh-so-many years ago. You were the one who encouraged me to write it down. Years later, you were the first person to whom I read the short story, which I kept working on, until ten years ago I told you, "This could be a book." And you told me to write it. And kept telling me. Once I had started in earnest, it was you who called me several times a week to see how the writing was coming and listened patiently while every chapter was read aloud. Even when you were exhausted from work, you listened. You prodded and poked in the most loving way. You believed in me, encouraged me, challenged me, were proud of me. You told me this often.

Thank you, my sister, from the bottom of my heart.

It matters to be thought of in a loving and healing way. Thank you to Bekki and Kristen, Marsha and Marc, Cherie, Beatriz, Ralph, Karen, Lexi, Paula, Dorothy, Lynda, John, Julie, Connie, Lana, and Marion. You have kept me in your hearts, left messages, checked in, and sent emails saying you believed in the story. You believed in me. Thoughts travel, and they reached me as I wrote, rewrote, tweaked, and untweaked. I knew you were a soft light, always encouraging, always on.

And finally, to all of you who love animals ~ thank you for the love you give to the four-legged teachers in our lives. Through their demonstration, they teach us to be better people.

A little book walks out into the world. Blessings to all who read and blessings to the little book on its way. Fini.

About the Author

Tian Wilson left home at 17 for college in Hawaii, the only state where she figured her Midwest parents couldn't drive to see her on the weekend. After sampling the offerings, she headed out into the world to begin her many lives. The first was in healthcare, which she loved except for allopathy's refusal to look at patients as people. After a few years of caring for elders, she began her long love affair with the written word—literally, as she was trained in the art of Calligraphy. From recreating old ninth-century manuscripts to teaching classes in various states in the Art of Lettering, she created a viable business that delighted the eye for over a decade.

An offer to play guitar and sing for a friend's wedding brought her to Albuquerque, NM, for the first time, where she stayed and began training as a Natural Therapeutic Specialist. For the next thirty years, both in NM and the Midwest, she worked with those in pain to provide bodywork, herbs, hydrotherapy, and what she calls "Basic Common Sense." During that time, she founded a massage therapy school in the Midwest, modeled after her alma mater in NM.

As time took its toll on hands and shoulders, she pivoted away from bodywork and trained in Laser Coaching from Master Coach, Marion Franklin. Which brings her to the current profession as she provides life and business coaching for her clients.

Life now includes authoring her first book: *Gifts From a Feral Cat: A Story of Love, Loss, and Miracles*. This book was written because she loves all God's critters, especially cats. And... she believes in miracles.